GW01460026

Dedicated to the rich history of Pensacola, "America's First Settlement",

to

My great great grandparents, George and Clara Barkley,

and to

My mother Rosalie Willis Tate and
Beloved aunt Adelaide Rutherford Willis
Whose passion for history and family compelled this book

GWT

"There is a history in all men's lives."

– William Shakespeare

BARKLEY HOUSE VIGNETTES:
PEOPLE AND EVENTS OF OLD PENSACOLA

FOREWORD

Why would anyone want to read about an old house? Indeed, what are "Barkley House Vignettes?"

Arguably the most historic structure in "America's First Settlement", Pensacola's Barkley House surely saw history played out within it's walls and upon its broad verandahs. This is not a history of the house, for the University of West Florida's esteemed Archaeology Institute has done extensive and rigorous study of the house itself. This book, instead, seeks to provide a glimpse backward to people and events, some well known, others not, who played out their roles in the rich gumbo of Pensacola history upon the stage of the Barkley House; once called "the official residence of Pensacola." Their past is our prologue.

Many of the historic *personae* herein left few footprints in the sands of time, and because of fragmentary records we are summoned to use our imaginations to flesh out some of the images drawn herein. In no way however does that mental extrapolation invalidate the facts we *do* have; it merely challenges us leave our 21st century frame of reference behind and soar on the magic carpet of the mind back into the world of George and Clara Barkley and their associates on the Florida frontier.

Some may criticize the lack of footnotes. With the caveat that this is not intended as a history text *per se*, I have provided instead a bibliography of sources for those demanding scholarly proof of the materials herein. It was my belief that flitting between text and footnotes might make the flow of the material more choppy, thus distracting the reader from simply enjoying the stories themselves. These vignettes of Pensacola history are designed to be of interest to serious scholar and layman alike, and every effort has been made to build these stories of people and events of early Pensacola upon a solid base of fact drawn from these bibliographic sources.

Many illustrations are employed to "connect the dots" and help form the mental pictures alluded to above. They do not always specifically depict "people and events of old Pensacola", but sometimes push the reader outward to a broader frame of reference. The captions are especially important as summaries and links to the main text.

If *"All the world's a stage and all the men and women merely players"*, as Shakespeare reminded us, let us part the curtain and enjoy this look back in time at the players who trod the stage of Pensacola's revered Barkley House!

GWT

BARKLEY HOUSE VIGNETTES:

PEOPLE AND EVENTS OF OLD PENSACOLA

The Barkleys and Their House; Scions of Pensacola's Past. The Creole elegance of Pensacola's historic Barkley House silently testifies to the sophistication and taste of its early occupants, London born merchant George W. Barkley and his French bride, Clara Garnier Barkley. Their elegant home, one of Pensacola's finest in it's day and allegedly it's first masonry residence, is now owned by the State of Florida and maintained and managed for benefit of all Floridians by West Florida Historic Preservation, Inc. West Florida Historic Preservation, Inc is that arm of the University of West Florida charged with protecting the historic treasures which define the rich history of Pensacola, "America's First Settlement". As this is written Pensacola's Barkley House is nearing it's third century as a silent witness to Northwest Florida's fascinating past.

Pensacola's most venerable historic residence, the Barkley House today is the flagship of UWF's historic preservation program, while in it's heyday, it was an important venue for history-shaping events. From their home beside the bay at 410 Florida Blanca Street, George and Clara Barkley observed and participated in some of the most notable events of the day; events affecting not only the dynamic city of Pensacola, but Territorial Florida, the young United States, and even across the ocean to political events in Europe. All the while young George Barkley made and eventually lost a fortune as a prominent merchant and bank president, held leadership appointments in the government of Pensacola and Florida militia, and helped found the revered Christ Church which still stands today, heralded as the oldest church in Florida. We honor the Barkley House today not just as a structure, but for what it stands for. We remember that while the people may be gone, the home stands sentinel, a tangible reminder of the remarkable convergence of people and events of almost two hundred years ago.

This retrospective then seeks to conceptualize Pensacola's beloved Barkley House as a stage upon which much of the history of their day played out. I felt, as a descendant of the Barkleys and a proud resident of Pensacola, that if I could know the feet which trod those floors at 410 Florida Blanca Street, eavesdrop on conversations long past, and come to know their essential human-ness, I could for all time and especially for today's generation, put the Barkleys and their historic home in proper perspective. To

1

the extent that they and their colleagues shaped the early destiny of Pensacola, theirs is a legacy which lives on today. As we shall see, that legacy is significant.

As our lives are today in 21st Century Pensacola, the Barkley's world was a network of intertwined relationships. A major purpose of this book then is to reweave the tapestry of their lives, and attempt in some small way to do for the Barkley's lives what the University of West Florida's archaeological research has done for their house. The Barkleys of Pensacola clearly hobnobbed with the elites of the day, consorting with a future president of the United States, the nephew of Emperor Napoleon I, and the closest living relative of George Washington. Because the entertaining of the day was based in the home, and the Barkley House was perhaps the most prominent residence in Pensacola, many historic guests likely graced the Barkley House itself. The Barkleys socialized and interacted with princes and princesses, a future president, congressmen, governors, mayors, key military figures, and prominent business and church leaders. They doubtless held lively discourse with political, social, and intellectual leaders of the era, such as Florida's first governor Andrew Jackson, it's subsequent acting governor George Walton II and would-be heirs to the throne of Napoleon Bonaparte. Last but not least, from the wide verandahs of Pensacola's Barkley House, they brokered the marriage of one of their daughters to a descendant of the family of George Washington, and through that connection linked both the Barkley family and Pensacola to many royal houses of Europe, all the way back to the Emperor Charlemagne, whom history regards as having given the first structure to modern day Europe. The history of the Pensacola Barkleys is truly a portal to world history.

Within these pages we shall attempt to paint a portrait of Pensacola's beloved Barkley House and of its rich history and the fascinating people who swirled in and around it. Some of the events described herein draw upon best-available historic fact, yet in the final analysis remain conjectural, obscured by the sands of time. Reconstructing this history of the Barkleys and their house is analogous to a court case for which the evidence is circumstantial, there being no witnesses to tell us what actually happened minute by minute. But court cases are routinely proven by circumstantial evidence, and we, too, are comfortable "proving" this history of the Barkleys and their house in that manner. A bibliography is identified for those demanding scholarly proof of these tales of the Barkleys and their house or simply seeking more detail. But part of the joy in this adventure is to exercise the mind by extrapolating the facts into a larger whole encompassing the Barkley era in old Pensacola; a sort of historical *gestalt*. For want of "witnesses" and/or a detailed written record, the tales herein require the reader to connect the historical dots provided by sparse records, and to transport themselves in imagination back to frontier Florida.

In this brief story of the Barkleys and their associates on the Florida frontier, we will use illustration to make more real for the reader the people and events described herein. Though we have a portrait of Madame Clara Garnier Barkley, tragically no known image of the protagonist, George W. Barkley survives. The reader is thus left to fashion that image of Barkley in imagination, dressed in the severe woolen clothing he would have brought from England, with stiff collared shirts, uncomfortable shoes, formal vests and hats, and other European accoutrements not at all appropriate to life in the hot, rustic, and altogether alien environment of the southern frontier, with it's sandspurs, snakes, mosquitoes, palmetto bugs, and other local "residents!"

Early Origins of the Barkley Family. As we shall show, George W. Barkley, whose name graces Pensacola's most historic home, was an immigrant from London, England, and descendant of the ancient Scottish Clan Barclay. Famed as discerning merchants and bankers, it was an ancestor, David Barclay who founded the famous Barclay's Bank of London on the Lombard Street property of his inlaws. Even earlier in time, the genealogist of today's Clan Barclay records that:

"The Scottish Barclays claim descent from Roger de Berchelai of Gloucestershire who was recorded in the Domesday Book in 1086 and who came to England with William the Conqueror. Sir Walter Barclay of Gartly, Lord of Redcastle and Inverkeillor was appointed Chamberlain of Scotland under William the Lion. The male line of Gartley ended with Walter, Canon of Moray in 1456. His sister married the Laird of Towie-Barclay and so the chiefship was carried into that house. The name was common throughout the 12th and 13th centuries in Kincardineshire and the East of Scotland. The Barclays of Mathers descend from Alexander de Berkeley, who married the heiress of Mathers in 1351. She was the sister of the Great Marischal of Scotland. Their descendants retained possession of these lands until David Barclay was forced to sell the estates for financial reasons in the 16th century. Another branch of the family, the Barclays of Urie are descended from Colonel David Barclay, one of a number of Scottish officers who had served in Sweden under Gustavus Adolphus. He acquired the Urie estate in 1647 and Robert his eldest son became a celebrated Quaker and was appointed Governor of East Jersey in 1682. There were several other important branches of the Barclay family including Collairnie in Fife, Pierston in Argyllshire and Tolly in Aberdeenshire. The Tolly branch obtained the estate about 1100 and it remained in the family until its sale by

the Honorable Charles Maitland Barclay of Tillycoultry, who married the last heiress Isabel Barclay in 1752. It was from this family that the famous Russian general, Field Marshal Prince Barclay de Tolly was descended. He was Minister of War during the Napoleonic invasion which was defeated in 1812. He died shortly after in 1818. The present-day chief is descended from the Towie-Barclays."

The ancient Towie-Barclay castle in Aberdeenshire, Scotland is the ancestral home of the Clan Barclay, from which Pensacola's George W. Barkley descends. It can be regarded as the spiritual forerunner of Pensacola's Barkley House, which, as part of Historic Pensacola Village, is on the National Register of Historic Places.

George Barkley Arrives in America and Settles in Pensacola. The ink was hardly dry on the Constitution of the United States when George W. Barclay was born July 25, 1793 in London, England. Notice the traditional Scottish spelling of the name. It was not until his immigration to the United States that he Americanized the spelling to "Barkley", the name by which we know his home in Pensacola of the 21st Century. As a timeline reference, when Barkley was born, George Washington was still president of the United States, Mozart was at the height of his musical genius, and it would be another hundred years before Monet would paint the water lilies of his garden at Giverney. Napoleon had not yet come to power, or brought to power with him the cast of powerful supporters whom the fates would later

4

connect to George Barkley himself. That connection between Barkley and the family of Napoleon would happen in a faraway frontier town on the hotly contested southern frontier of the US; Pensacola, America's first settlement and the City of Five Flags. At the time of his birth, George Barkley's adopted homeland of the United States of America had been constituted only five years earlier, in 1787, with the drafting of the US Constitution in Philadelphia. It would be an altogether correct perception to observe that George W. Barkley and the United States grew up together.

At age 26, the young Barkley left familiar England and sailed for the fledgling United States. His port of arrival was Baltimore, where on May 3, 1819 he renounced his loyalties to the crown of England and swore out an oath of intent to become a citizen of the United States. This act was more than symbolic. American distrust of the British still ran deep, for another timeline of history reminds us that they had attacked our capital city and burned the White House just a few years before. Signing over his British citizenship irrevocably cast the fate of George Barkley with the still insecure United States, whose future, despite the successful American Revolution, was still in doubt as the great European powers jockied for influence in a global chess game manipulated from across the Atlantic.

Though the record is silent, it is likely that George Barkley left his British homeland because of the strict laws of primogeniture still prevalent there. From a practical standpoint, primogeniture meant that his older brother Walter would inherit the family fortune, leaving the ambitious young George with nothing more than the family's good name. With a good mercantile and banking background, a sense of adventure, opportunities beckoning from across the Atlantic, and deprived of any inheritance in England, George Barkley sought his fortunes in the brave new world of United States of America.

Opportunity in the new nation was a siren call. It was free from Britain, thanks to the success of the American Revolution. It welcomed all who would heed its message of the infinite political wisdom and unprecedented freedoms offered by the US Constitution. And recent expansion resulting from Napoleon's sale to the US of the vast Louisiana Territory promised riches which which were still only vaguely understood. With Europe's centuries old traditions and rigid autocratic governments still largely in place and stifling, it is easy to understand how exciting the unfettered promise of America must have appeared by comparison.

George Barclay immigrated to the US in 1819, renounced his British citizenship, and Americanized his name from the Scottish "Barclay" to "Barkley".

Transiting briefly through Baltimore, Barkley settled first in New Orleans, where he met another recent immigrant family, the Garnier's of France; father John Garnier, his recent American bride Ann, sons Charles and John, Jr., and daughters Clara Louise and Rosa. At that time several still affected their French names; Jean, Claire, and Rose instead of John, Clara, and Rosa as they were later Americanized. During his short stay in New Orleans George Barkley's ties to the Garniers grew, and included the beginnings of a long-term financial relationship between the younger Garnier, Charles, and Barkley, who at the time were both in their mid-twenties. More significantly, the stunningly beautiful dark eyed Garnier daughter, Clara, first captured the attentions of George Barkley during this transitional period in New Orleans.

Sparse records suggest that the Garniers were political refugees from post Napoleonic France, and may have become a target of the "White Terror" about 1815, when pro-Bourbon royalists roamed throughout France seeking retribution for some of Napoleon's excesses. The Garniers intentionally led a low-profile life in the new world with few records available to substantiate their flight from France, for fear of reprisals both here and for family members who remained on the continent.

Clara Louise Garnier was born Claire Louise Garnier in Bordeaux, France circa 1800. She immigrated to the fledgling United States in 1819-20 with her widowed father and two brothers. Claire Americanized her name to Clara and married George W. Barkley in Pensacola June 25, 1822. This image is from a miniature painted on ivory in her home, Bordeaux, France, at about age 18.

When George Barkley settled in Pensacola we must remind ourselves that it would still be decades until the new United States of America effectively stretched "from sea to shining sea." The great western and northern expanses gained by the Louisiana Purchase remained unsettled wilderness. Still largely an Atlantic seaboard power, the new nation urgently needed to rid itself of the latent threats along its southern frontier where it shared a common boundary with potentially hostile European powers. It also sought in the early 1800's to acquire ports along the Gulf of Mexico which would facilitate trade to the south with Latin America while preventing those ports from becoming beachheads of foreign influence. The port of Pensacola was a special prize. Dominated at one time or another by English, French, and Spanish suitors, it was neglected by all and desperately needed a change.

Into this mix was thrust the person of Andrew Jackson, a near cult figure of his day. In *Pensacola: Spaniards to Space Age* historian Virginia Parks states categorically that "*The Americanization of Pensacola resulted from the ambitions of one man; Andrew Jackson.*" More than any other man, it was he who was the agent and guardian of American interests on the southern frontier.

Concurrently Spanish King Ferdinand VII was experiencing troubles at home and shrunken influence abroad. The British lost their foothold along the Gulf Coast at the Battle of New Orleans, literally smashed by Jackson's audacious leadership and his rag tag band of Americans. As a supposed settlement of the French and Indian War, the Treaty of Paris, February 10, 1763, gave all of North America east of the Mississippi, other than New Orleans, to the British. The French also turned over their claims of New Orleans and the lands west of the Mississippi to Spain, as compensation for Spain's surrendering Florida to the British. Though this appeared to put French interests in North America in eclipse, the native American population continued to oppose the British, and even without affirmative political control, France continued to exert *de facto* influence in the new world. Francophile populations persisted both in the north, in Canada, in the major centers of Quebec and Montreal and along the Saint Lawrence seaway, and in the far south, along the Gulf Coast, in such places as Biloxi, Mobile, and New Orleans. While history may record that officially the French lost the French and Indian War, they had the last laugh, retaining their influence, if not autonomous rule, in those locales. The British, meanwhile, were forcibly ejected from North America once and for all by the War of 1812.

After the War of 1812, a combination of political maneuvering, military sabre-rattling, and a determination by the US Congress to bring the Florida territory into the US orbit seemed certain to end the Spanish occupation. In these heady times along the Gulf Coast, George Barkley no doubt saw the opportunity of pending annexation of Florida into the United States as ripe for personal fortune making. We do not know why the restless young Barkley left New Orleans, but it quite possibly was the offer of employment for the records next show that he settled in Pensacola in 1820, with appointment as Customs Inspector for the burgeoning port. Whatever the reason, it was fortuitous for Pensacola and for the young Barkley, who went on to become a highly successful merchant, auctioneer, shipping company owner, warehouseman, owner of a reading and news room, bank president, church leader, city treasurer and tax collector, and pillar of the community. Still facing uncertainties with Seminole tribes to the east, Barkley also received appointment as a major in the First Brigade of Florida Militia, serving as brigade quartermaster. It would be no overstatement to say that he was one of the most influential of all early Pensacolains.

George Barkley's French Colleagues, the Garniers, and Their Move to Pensacola. Several of the Garniers whom Barkley had befriended in New Orleans also moved to Pensacola, where they were destined to become allied in both marriage and business with George W. Barkley. John Garnier, Jr. and his brother Charles, however, remained in New Orleans where Charles had both a law practice and other business interests. Extensive records show that he and John Jr. profited from Louisiana's plantation economy as commission merchants, brokering cotton shipments from upriver and in return supplying plantation owners the supplies, equipment, and luxuries that supported their lavish lifestyles. Both of the Garnier sons married there; John Jr. to Lubin and Charles to Sophie, both of whose maiden names are unknown. In 1817 John Jr. purchased a fine residence from Mme. FranAnoise Desuau Delacroix at 718 St. Peter Street restored in the 1920's by architect Richard Koch and since 1933 the venue for the popular Pat O'Briens lounge. That early date of 1817 suggests that the Garnier family spent several years in New Orleans before John, Sr. and his daughters pushed onward to Pensacola in 1820-21.

We know that the elder Garnier, John, (perhaps still affecting the French spelling, Jean) together with wife Ann and daughters Clara and Rosa, moved to Pensacola at about the same time as George Barkley, early enough to be in the city for the 1821 change of flags from Spain to the United States. The old governmental structure of East and West Florida as had been used by the Spanish remained in effect until the two were merged into the single US Territory of Florida, with it's capital at Pensacola, and placed under the governorship of Andrew Jackson. Though Pensacola had deteriorated under lax Spanish rule, Barkley had the insight to look beyond it's rustic crudeness to a brighter day under US rule. The end of Spanish neglectful occupation filled the air with excitement and possibility. As the date for ending Spain's rule approached, young Pensacola was filled with speculators, office seekers, and opportunists, among whom was George Barkley. His confidence in Pensacola was not misplaced.

As we look back into these early days of territorial Florida, it is well to remember that there was only scant exploration and only a few primitive settlements south of about the 30th parallel, with the capital at Pensacola dominating affairs of the territory. The populous tourism-dominated Florida peninsula to the south as we know it today was not even a dream, much less a reality.

Though small, with a population of less than 1,000, Pensacola in the early 1820's was the most prominent city in Florida. Spanish East and West Florida's were merged under the temporary governorship of Andrew Jackson in 1821.

At the time George Barkley and the Garnier family arrived in Pensacola, however, before it was named by the US as the territory's capital city, it was a rustic, largely dilapidated frontier military outpost, controlled at various times by the French, British, and Spanish. It was then and is now situated strategically on one of the finest harbors in America. We know from records that both George Barkley and John Garnier, spurred on by the excitement of impending American rule, had settled in Pensacola by 1821 and, though we lack documentation, it is a virtual certainty that both the Garniers and George Barkley were witnesses to history near present day Pensacola's Plaza

Ferdinand when Andrew Jackson accepted the Florida Territory from Spain on that steamy day of July 17, 1821, concluding a purchase for which the US paid some $5 million dollars to the crown of Spain, via the Adams-Onis Treaty. According to markers located behind today's T.T. Wentworth Museum, it is likely that the actual ceremony of transfer from Spain to the United States took place at the old Spanish garrison. Behind the T.T. Wentworth Museum today the old brick foundations provide evocative reminders of this momentous Spanish colonial period in Gulf Coast history. Spain's legacy also of course lives on in the street names of Pensacola's historic district.

Representing US President John Adams, Andrew Jackson and the Spanish "landlord", Governor Callava, signed the formal documents of transfer at the garrison, after which the flag of Spain was doused and that of the United States hoisted, signalling the transfer and giving the U.S. uncontested dominion over the entirety of Florida for the first time. Spain's reluctance to turn over the valuable Florida territory was manifest in the hostility between Governor Callava and Andrew Jackson at the time of the ceremony. A 21 gun salute was fired by the American warship USS HORNET in Pensacola Roads, and the "Star Spangled Banner" floated over Florida for the first time on that hot and humid July afternoon.

In that act, the curtain came down forever on foreign colonization of America's southern frontier, and the threats to US sovereignty they represented. Previously contested among British, French, and Spanish overlords, Pensacola would forever flourish beneath the security of the Stars and Stripes…and George Barkley was there. In the act of transfer of the Florida Territory from Spain to the United States, Barkley's dreams moved a step closer to reality, as for the first time, young Pensacola became forever folded into the political stability, strategic security, and mercantile relationships of the United States.

George W. Barkley, the Garniers, and Andrew Jackson. As up-and-coming community leaders it would be unlikely that Barkley and his soon-to-be in law John Garnier would miss such an event. The change of flags to cement the purchase of Florida from Spain proved as momentous for these pioneer Pensacola families as it did for the United States. One can imagine Barkley and Garnier trekking the sandy streets and sweltering in old-world clothing to see "Old Hickory" preside over the end of Spanish rule.

Andrew Jackson, one of the most illustrious figures in American and Pensacola history, accepted turnover of the Florida Territory from Spain in 1821 and served as first governor of the territory under US rule. In the tiny upper crust of Pensacola at that time, he was without doubt a colleague of both the Barkley and Garnier families. Jackson was also the political benefactor of Pensacola brick maker Byrd C. Willis and rewarded him with a patronage appointment at the Pensacola Navy Yard.

Appointed by President Monroe as acting governor of the Florida Territory as soon as he took possession from Spain, for a time Jackson and his raven-haired wife Rachel lived on Palafox Street near Plaza Ferdinand where the event took place. It is more than likely, in fact highly probable, that both Barkley and Garnier made the acquaintance of Andrew and Rachel Jackson. No doubt there was both a business relationship as well as a social one, quite likely at some of the balls and social events which Rachel found scandalous. No fan of the Pensacola social scene, which was as bawdy as any frontier town ever was, Rachel Jackson wrote frequently of her displeasure with the raucous, brawling, waterfront town. It is written that frontier Pensacola was so dilapidated after decades of Spanish neglect, that Andrew and Rachel Jackson refused to live in the "government house". Rachel Jackson described Pensacola as *"rowdy, heathen, with dilapidated buildings and a polyglot population."* While a resident, she wrote that *"The inhabitants all speak Spanish and French, Some four or five languages. Such a mixed multitude you, nor any of us, ever had idea of. Fewer white people by far than any other...Seamen strolled with knives in their belts and coins burning in their pockets; absurd little Spanish soldiers; yellow women with well turned limbs and insinuating glances; Jamaican blacks bearing prodigious burdens on their heads; a grandee in his carriage. And must I say, the worst people here are the cast-off Americans."* Such was the world into which the well bred Barkley brought his aristocratic French-born wife.

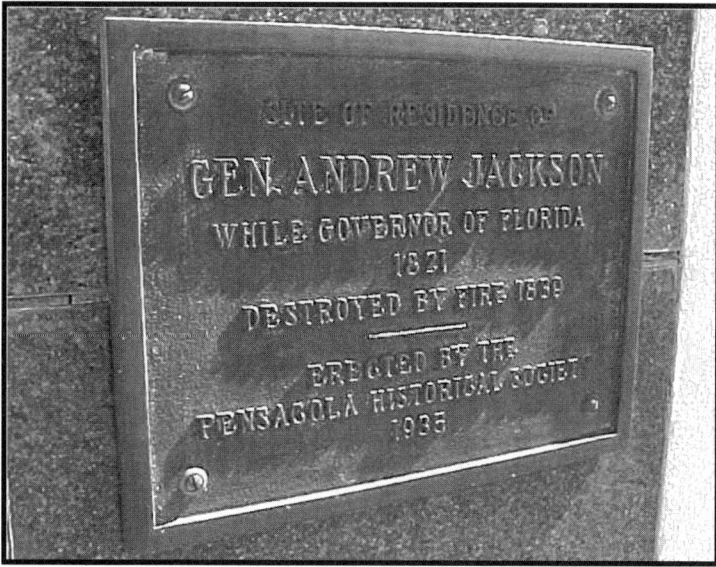

Andrew and Rachel Jackson lived on Palafox Street when he served as governor of the newly acquired Florida Territory.

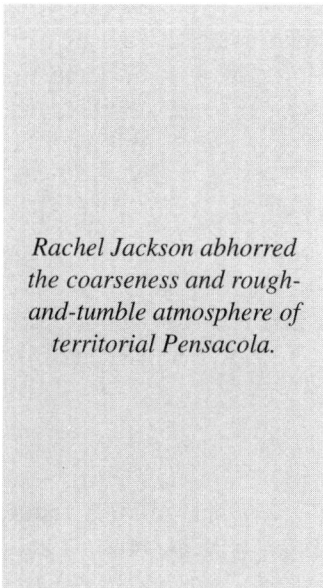

Rachel Jackson abhorred the coarseness and rough-and-tumble atmosphere of territorial Pensacola.

According to best-available information, there were only 695 residents of Pensacola at the time of the change of flags, thus it is a virtual certainty that George Barkley and the Garnier family knew Andrew and Rachel Jackson well during Jackson's tenure as acting governor. Many of those 695 residents were Spanish holdovers no longer in power, many were slaves, some were free men of color; a status conferred by the Spanish. Because there were few white settlers and even fewer in positions of authority, it is reasonable to state with some certainty that there was only a tiny circle of community leaders, of whom Jackson, Barkley, and John Garnier were a part. Evidence of this relationship, especially as regards John Garnier, is found in *The Florida Historical Quarterly*, which reports that Andrew Jackson appointed John Garnier as a Justice of the Peace on July 17, 1821, the same day he became acting governor. Other prominent Pensacola names are contained in the same Jacksonian appointment announcement; John Innerarity, Henry Breckenridge, John Brosnaham, and others. Certainly Garnier was among the leaders and in this appointment is clear evidence of a pre-existing relationship of trust and confidence between Garnier and Andrew Jackson. It also hints at a possible legal background for Garnier, though he never practiced law here so far as we know. He is, nevertheless, referred to in some sources as "Judge Garnier."

Though President James Monroe had appointed Andrew Jackson commissioner of the United States, with the powers of governor when he accepted title of the Florida Territory from Spain, Jackson left Pensacola just four months after the change of flags. His imprint and legacy on Pensacola were nevertheless enormous, far out of proportion to the short time he held office. First and foremost of course, he presided over the transfer of power from Spain ending forever the revolving door of European control of the Gulf coast region. Having secured American interests thusly, Andrew Jackson served as the Florida Territory's first governor. Even earlier he had, with some controversy, put down the Indian rebellions in northwest Florida. Reacting to latent threats from covetous foreign powers, and in a move to solidify the recently announced Monroe Doctrine of hemispheric power, Jackson saw to strengthening Pensacola's fortifications, laid the groundwork for it's venerable Navy Yard, and established the first functioning US governmental structure over the previously French, English, and Spanish territory.

Doubtless during Andrew Jackson's tenure here, important citizens such as George W. Barkley and John Garnier would have shared their visions for Pensacola's future with the man who would in a few years become president of the United States. We know from *Territorial Papers of the Florida Territory* that they were both politically active based on appointments to various government posts and both Barkley and Garnier's names appear on several political petitions; to the President of the United States supporting Colonel James Gadsden to replace William DuVal as governor, petitions concerning a postmaster, and petitions concerning the port of Pensacola.

In another wrinkle of fate, based on his experiences in Pensacola Andrew Jackson would later reward a political crony, Colonel Byrd Charles Willis of Virginia, with a presidential appointment as his agent at the newly established Pensacola Navy Yard. In turn, that set in motion Willis's historic connection to the Barkley family, which led in time to both business dealings and the important family intermarriage of a Willis heir to a Barkley daughter. Andrew Jackson himself was responsible for Colonel Willis's presence in Pensacola, and it is, as we shall see later, though Willis that Pensacola and the Barkley family are linked to the family of George Washington and to European royalty.

Barkley and Garnier Ties Grow. The strengthening relationship between the immigrants who had met in New Orleans, the French Garniers and English George Barkley was also momentous. In May 1822, Barkley borrowed a sum of "seed money" from John Garnier's son, Charles, who had remained in New Orleans when the rest of the Garniers moved to Pensacola. In an entry dated May 12, 1822, in Book A Page 51 of the Escambia County deed book is found a record of a lien Charles Garnier held on George Barkley for a "*large sum of money loaned about May 1822.*" With borrowed Garnier seed-money, George Barkley embarked on what would be a long and lucrative succession of merchant interests in Pensacola. But greater still, the romantic interest between George Barkley and the strikingly beautiful Clara Garnier, which had begun two years earlier in New Orleans, blossomed. This romance would forever link the destinies of the two immigrant families in ways which neither could have foreseen, and set the stage for the couple's ownership of the home which now proudly wears their name…Pensacola's historic Barkley House.

It is said that initially John Garnier disapproved mightily of his daughter's affections for the successful merchant George Barkley. Barkley, he complained, lacked the credentials of European aristocracy which he felt were appropriate for his daughter. Barkley was a "mere merchant" seeking the affections of French nobility, which is how the elder Garnier still perceived himself. But love will triumph, and on June 25, 1822, the dark-eyed brunette beauty Clara Louise Garnier, *ex* of Bordeaux, married George W. Barkley *ex* of London, in Pensacola, during the days immediately following Pensacola's Spanish occupation, and with the storm clouds of the Garnier's turbulent French homeland just over the horizon. With their marriage began the unique intersection of lives, cultures, events, and places which we explore in this book.

The Ups and Downs of George W. Barkley. As we have alluded to above, George Barkley arrived in Pensacola powered by the genes of the long-successful Barclay family of England and Scotland. His genetic predispositions and the early business knowledge he had acquired in England prepared him well for entrepreneurship on the Florida frontier. Using the seed money borrowed from his brother-in-law Charles Garnier, George Barkley's business acumen, no doubt acquired from generations of Scottish Barclay enterprise, rose to the fore. His store stocked with Garnier-financed goods flourished. Ever seeking the lucrative opportunity, George Barkley also turned to auctioneering, specializing in tobacco which was being cultivated experimentally in the area. He advertised his store heavily, luring townspeople to buy his stocks of groceries, wine, champagne, tea and coffee, hardware, fabrics, and accoutrements for the home, such as lamp oil. Sketchy evidence suggests that he was assisted in merchandising his wares by his father-in-law, John Garnier, for whom a mercantile career was a rude transition after his earlier life of French aristocracy.

JUST received and for sale low for cash,

14 hhds. New-Orleans SUGAR.
6 bbls.   do. Refined Loaf Sugar.
20 barrels Whiskey.
5   do.   Monongahela.
20 do.   superior Flour.
20 do.   Prime and Mess Pork.
10 do.   Molasses.
6   do.   Onions.
20 half barrels family Mess Beef.
5 barrels White Beans.
27 boxes Porter.
20 dozen Scotch Ale.
30 kegs Lard.
10 bags Rio Coffee.
4000 family Canvassed Hams.
And a large and general assortment of Glass and Crockery Ware.
                    GEO. W. BARKLEY.
August 19, 1837—24

George W. Barkley was one of territorial Pensacola's
most important merchants.

The Barkley emporium provided the essentials of life for the small and struggling town, as well as offering the few luxury goods that were available on the Florida frontier.

PICKLES, CATSUP'S & SAUCES.—
54 boxes assorted, just received from
Boston, via Mobile, consisting of

Gerkins,
Cucumbers,
Percolily,   } Pickles.
Onions,
Walnuts.

Tomato,
Mushroon,   } Catsups.
Walnut,

Red Currant Jelly,
Cranberry Jam,
Raspberry Jam.

GEO. W. BARKLEY.
March 3, 1838.   58

Noting that Pensacola's crude road system limited commerce between the port city and her neighbors, George Barkley acquired a sloop YANKEE, mortgaged to him by Hamilton Smith for $180, and schooner, ALEXANDER OF PENSACOLA, purchased in Appalachicola for $2,000 for transport of the wares of the city's brickyards and lumberyards to markets along the coast. A bill of sale dated Feb 9, 1838 describes the ALEXANDER OF PENSACOLA as a two masted square-stern schooner of 64 feet 8 inches length, displacing seventy and 12/95 tons. Her master Alexander Lamb, for whom she was presumably named, reported that she was built near Pensacola in 1837. Again, Barkley's father-in-law John Garnier assisted him in his shipping, stevedoring, and warehousing interests. The privately owned Barkley Wharf was a commercial asset of importance to the city, and was located near the site of the Barkley House along the bay shore, an area recorded on some maps as "Barkley Point". As Barkley's businesses thrived and his prominence in the city grew, he was appointed by Mayor Charles Evans to important city administrative positions including, according to an article in the Pensacola *Gazette* dated July 31, 1824, those of treasurer and tax collector. No doubt these important civic duties were based upon financial knowledge acquired from family-based enterprises, including the famous Barclay's Bank of London. Positions of trust and leadership in the young city of Pensacola assure us that George Barkley had quickly earned his way into prominence. In addition to his financial credentials we may be certain that his position in the growing community was buttressed by his reputation for dependability and scrupulous honesty, traits which would later be eulogized in his obituary.

The Barkley's and Slavery. Though it was seen as a legitimate business interest in the 1830's and 40's, the stain of slavery darkens our present-day interpretation of George Barkley and his Garnier in-laws. There is evidence that Barkley was not only a slave owner, but bought and sold slaves for profit as well. His first slaves, Lucy and Billy, were purchased in 1824 from Oliver Clark for $250 each. Billy carried the curious nickname of "Billy Chicken", which some believe to have been a reference to his conduct of cock-fights, for it was a popular sport of the day. In an interesting example of the dichotomy of the day regarding slavery, the 1830 Pensacola census records that the household of John Garnier, Barkley's father-in-law late of France, contained BOTH one male slave and one free woman of color! Ambivalence about the controversial right of one human being to own another can surely be seen in that data!

Clara Garnier Barkley's New Orleans brother Charles was also a slave trader, and there are multiple records of his slave transactions as well. For at least this writer, this casts doubt on the sincerity of his belief in "Liberte, Egalite, Fraternite" preached so passionately in his homeland during the French Revolution. In one transaction Charles Garnier purchased a Negro woman named Hannah and her seven year old daughter Charlotte from John Woodfolk of Augusta, Georgia for $600. He then presented the two as "gifts" to his Pensacola sister Clara Garnier Barkley on December 29, 1824, so she too bears censure as a slave owner. While we today tend to view slavery as a purely racist activity of white over black, Deed Book A discloses that one Frasina Henar, a Pensacola free woman of color, sold to Charles Garnier "a Negro slave named George, about fifty years old. In early Pensacola, slave traders of all races engaged in the heinous and controversial practice for their personal gain!

Other slaves of the Barkley household are documented in George W. Barkley's last will and testament, which discloses:

*"Mulatto boy William, aged about 32 years, appraised $200; Negro girl Anne $600, and Negro boy Dick appraised $250."* Census and tax data throughout the period 1830 until the time of his death in 1854, along with his last will and testament, provide additional evidence of George Barkley's traffic in slaves and his unabashed use of slave labor at his home and businesses. He died a decade before the Emancipation Proclamation would yield their freedom, so while from the 21st century we look with disdain on his slave interests, our criticism must be tempered with realization that it was a legal enterprise in his day.

Beginning in 1823 George Barkley's name appear eighteen times on the Escambia County Deed Books, for slaves, schooners, land, and appointment as auctioneer.

Barkley and the Real Estate Boom. Anticipating the coming growth of the city when it was to become capital of West Florida, Barkley sought to capitalize on the real estate frenzy created by the transfer of flags from Spain. Perhaps it was this opportunity which induced him, like many, to move to Pensacola in the first place. His first ventures were to acquire land as the Spanish left the city, often at tax sales when former Spanish landowners, no longer in power or even welcome, simply walked away from their properties. This was a fitting turn of the historic wheel, for the Spanish had condemned all land ownership by non-Spanish citizens when they took control of the city from the British in 1781. Easy come; easy go.

In this manner in 1823 George Barkley acquired 130 English arpents of land from departed Spanish landowner Vincente Ordozgoity, followed in the next few years by several lots in town, platted originally under the British. Other land records show the continuance of land transactions by Barkley from Spanish residents perhaps at the time of their departure after turnover from Spain to the US; Joaquin de Osorno (a high government official) and Antonio Montero, to name but two.

Much of the land ownership in very early Pensacola, during British and Spanish occupation, was connected with the Panton Leslie-John Forbes Company under the adroit leadership of John Innerarity. Innerarity was a business and social colleague of George Barkley's and was also of Scottish descent. Much of the land which George Barkley acquired, including several of the lots he would eventually build on was connected with the Panton Leslie-John Forbes enterprise. The Panton Leslie-John Forbes venture is well documented as Pensacola's foremost company of its day, with huge interests all along the central Gulf Coast. It thrived as an Indian trading company and land empire in the lush corruption of the Spanish occupation.

John Innerarity was apparently the quintessential wheeler-dealer and in settling the estates of William Panton and John Leslie, liquidated the assets of their company in any way that he could. On behalf of the company, Innerarity sold Lot 31, as platted by the British years before and titled to Beltram Souchet, to Colonel William Barnet. Barkley in turn bought Lot 31, at the corner of Florida Blanca and Zaragossa Streets, from Barnet for $500 in 1825. It evidently had a small wooden house on it, and Barkley may have even resided there for a time, but there is no documentation of that. Between 1825 and 1828, he added lots 26, 27, and 30. George Barkley through these years continued to deal extensively with his brother-in-law Charles Garnier of New Orleans, and it was through this means that on September 17, 1835 Barkley paid him $500 for lot 25 on the bay front. Aggregated together these lots provided a large and well-sited homestead by the bay for George and Clara Barkley.

Though he retained these lots for his own use, Barkley's hoped-for fortune in real estate speculation was not to be, thwarted when in 1824 the territorial capital was relocated from Pensacola to Tallahassee. At the time Tallahassee was a mere patch of desolate piney woods, but located centrally between Pensacola on the territory's west and Saint Augustine on it's east. Such a location avoided issues of favoritism of east over west, and provided a practical halfway meeting point for the new territorial legislature, though it was a disaster for investors in Pensacola. Land speculation had been a chief occupation in Pensacola but when the capital was moved away the speculative real estate boom collapsed. Real estate investor Barkley must have been sorely disappointed as he watched his hoped-for real estate fortune slip through his fingers like snow-white Pensacola sand.

Conjecture About the Origins of the Barkley House. Speculation and rumor hold many theories of the original construction of the Barkley House, including a fanciful notion that it was part of the British garrison before 1781. Others believe it to have been associated with the Spanish occupation and believe that it originally featured tunnels from the house to the area which is now Seville Square. None of these theories have been proven, yet they persist in local lore and legend. Some local residents describe having played in the tunnel(s) as children, yet no proof of their existence is forthcoming. Was this the active imagination of childhood talking? Or is the "Barkley House tunnel" one more fact now concealed, quite literally, by the sands of time? Until a full scientific archaeological study of the existence of tunnels confirms or refutes them, we are left to ponder the possibilities, intrigued by fanciful rumors and legend. Given the sandy, unstable soil of the area, in all likelihood the Barkley tunnels existed only in the active imaginations of Pensacola children of a bygone age.

As to the house itself, the evidence shows that Barkley himself built it between 1825 and the early 1830's, and probably with at least some brick from a colleague's brickyard. That colleague actually intermarried into the Barkley family, raising the likelihood that they may have collaborated on the Barkley House's construction. This heretofore unpublished theory is supported by several salient facts, yet in the final analysis, is dependent upon a certain amount of conjecture. That said, the theory which follows rests on facts which while tangential to the actual act of construction, at least support the notion that Barkley built the house. Once again we are tantalized with sketchy circumstantial evidence, and a paucity of fact. These evidentiary problems are also faced by other theories concerning the home's construction.

It is known that George W. Barkley shipped bricks in the late 1820's and 30's for the brickyard owned jointly by Jacksonian political appointee in Pensacola, Colonel Byrd Charles Willis and his partner, Prussian immigrant Henry Slaback. Their brickyard was located a few miles north of the commercial heart of Pensacola, in the vicinity of Gull Point on Mackey Bay. (Somewhere in time that name was mis-transposed. It appears on 1835 maps as Gulf Point rather than Gull Point.)

Barkley was both a social and business colleague of Willis, but the strongest evidence of the strength of the relationship of the two comes in the fact that the families intermarried. One of the Barkley daughters married Willis's grandson, named Byrd Charles for his grandfather. Clearly between 1825 and 1835, as Barkley's wealth and status grew, at the very time he was contemplating a suitable residence for his family, he and Willis were close associates, and their families enjoyed warm personal relations leading ultimately to intermarriage.

Would it not have made sense for Barkley to build with bricks from the brickyard of his friend, business associate, and future in-law? The timing for such a theory is perfect, as it is believed that the Barkley House was built between 1825 and 1830, which was the heyday of the Willis brickyard venture, and a time when Willis and Barkley did considerable business together. Some have theorized that the Barkley House is much older than Barkley's occupancy in the early 1830's, and support this theory with studies showing that the Barkley House was built of "scrap brick", noting that there are seven different sizes of brick in the structure. This theory holds that the brick of the house was cannibalized from earlier Spanish, French, or English structures on or near the site.

Using the same fact, however, of multiple types of brick, it is equally plausible that George Barkley was aided by a business and social colleague and future in-law. The individual in question, Colonel Byrd Charles Willis, owned a brickyard and might well have aided Barkley by selling or giving him, in addition to first quality bricks, those that were considered "seconds" from Willis' Scenic Heights brickyard. Willis did a huge business with the Federal government providing brick for Pensacola's fortifications, and those not meeting standards for construction of forts might have still been quite adequate for house construction. The multiple bricks of the Barkley House might therefore be a helping hand from a friend, and neither proves nor denies that the house was constructed earlier or with brick from old colonial fortifications. Adding to the plausibility of the Willis brick theory, we know that Barkley's ships frequently carried his friend Willis's bricks to market and construction sites, and would have passed close by Barkley Point and the commercial wharf there.

Though absolute ironclad proof is lacking that George W. Barkley built the residence we now revere, it seems the most plausible and the above theory is both feasible and likely. Connecting the bits of fragmentary evidence, even if one disallows the new theory above regarding construction from Willis Brickyard materials, we can note that:

1. The recorded prices which George Barkley paid for the lots upon which the Barkley House stands would have been inadequate for property with a fine brick home, so he likely was the original builder, and

2. Barkley had social, business, and later family relationships with a well-known brickyard owner whose bricks he transported to market.

3. We can speculate with near 100% certainty that it was indeed George Barkley who built today's historic National Registry "Barkley House", possibly of a combination of available brick cannibalized from older construction near the site, and perhaps augmented with new brick from his friend's brickyard.

The House. Built to catch the cooling breezes from the bay, The Barkley House is a classic "Creole High House", perhaps the finest example of that style in Florida. With sturdy thick walls (16 inches tapering to 12 inches) of porous brick endemic to the sandy-soils of the area, it is coated in whitewashed stucco bearing a grooved ashlar pattern reminiscent of Mount Vernon, but on a much smaller scale. According to the documents submitted to register the house as a national landmark, it is the oldest masonry house in Pensacola. With the main house having dimensions of 56'2" X 42'2", it's two story main living areas rest over a flush on grade English basement. A fine gabled roof with three dormers per side gives the roof its distinctive appearance.

Entering the central hall, two large rooms on either side each contain fireplaces set in plastered chimneys. Floors are tongue-in-groove pine throughout. There were a total of ten rooms above grade in the original house; five each on the first and second floors. Eight had fireplaces.

To the southeast of the original house was a kitchen annex or "summer kitchen" which was evidently a replica of the main house, along with the cooks quarters. Tragically, as often happened with such kitchens, it has succumbed to fire.

There was also a two bedroom annex on the northeast side of the house, likely for slave quarters. All of these were joined by covered verandahs over ten foot walkways underneath. The ample yard consisting of several contiguous lots sloped toward the bay where "one could pass the carriage house and boat house on the way to the (commercial Barkley) wharf." The house as we see it today is substantially closer to the water due to erosion along the bay front. All in all, Barkley Point was home to a residential and commercial spread of near-estate proportions, and more aptly described as a complex of buildings than just the single residence extant today.

The original furnishings of the Barkley House have been swallowed up by the intervening years, and we are left to envision the likely combination of furniture styles the Barkley's might have used. In all likelihood a few French pieces imported by the Garniers of Bordeaux aristocracy were used at the Barkley House at 410 Florida Blanca Street. These would have perhaps been balanced by George Barkely's predispositions for things English, and articles acquired in the course of his mercantile business, of American manufacture. Despite Madame Clara Garnier Barkley's aristocratic French heritage, no evidence whatsoever exists to support a view that she furnished her home in the high French fashion so popular in the salons of Mobile and New Orleans; in fact quite the opposite. A working family home, Pensacola's Barkley House was far less ornate and it's furnishings relatively Spartan by comparison, determined by availability in the still-rustic Pensacola of sand streets and small population.

It is a rewarding experience to recreate in one's mind the ambience of the house in its heyday. Though a large home by the standards of the day, there would be a certain hustle and bustle. Nine Barkley children, the two parents, a few slaves, and a stream of visitors assured a sense that this house was very lived in. As afternoon faded into twilight, the family would sit in clothing we would classify today as rather formal on the wide south veranda and watch the sun turn the western skies to rosy mauve; clouds catching the last light of another Pensacola day and reflecting in the still waters of the bay. The children would be playing, laughing, running, and tumbling about on the broad lawn...then several hundred yards wider on the bayside of the house than the setting we see today. George and Clara would chat with neighbors until called in by live-in slave Lucy for dinner, then would retire to the home's rather dark interior, with deep blue and green painted walls, to its candle or oil lamp lit dining room. After dinner, in deep shadows cast by a few candles and oil lamps, daughter Lucy Rose Barkley would play her beloved piano for the entertainment of all, as George sipped on a glass of port, recently brought from New Orleans by his sloop YANKEE, while Clara did needlepoint in the dim light. With no window screens and of course lacking the luxury of 21st Century air conditioning, Pensacola's ubiquitous mosquitos buzzed and nipped in the quiet, as the voices of the younger children could be heard chattering from their bedrooms upstairs, squabbling as siblings have always done.

Today's structure at 410 Florida Blanca Street is but a portion of the original Barkley properties. Two wings to the east housing the kitchen and slave quarters burned. West Florida Historic Preservation, Inc. and the University of West Florida plan to reconstruct these portions of the historic Barkley property. Contemporaneous accounts from the Barkley era also describe a raised walkway down to his commercial wharf as well as a carriage house on the south side of the main house.

The overall effect of night time in early Pensacola was one of inky darkness. Inside the Barkley House there were only candles and kerosene lamps and the dark-painted walls absorbed most of their glow. Outside there were very few people about, and of course no traffic or street lights. The 1830's on the southern frontier were primitive indeed, and the atmosphere of the small city by the bay was harsh. Pensacola was a small dark town that generally went to sleep early, save for the few inebriated seamen who roamed the waterfront.

As the wind sprang up, George Barkley would walk out on the veranda straining to look across the darkened long lawns at his schooner ALEXANDER OF PENSACOLA tied alongside Barkley Wharf to be sure she would ride out the wind and tide in safety. One more trip to the outhouse before bed, then shoo away a fox sniffing around the enclosure where the family dog Addie had just given birth to a litter of fine pups. Prayers were said, as the Barkley family thanked God for one more day passed in old Pensacola, put on night caps, and slid under the mosquito netting of their bed. Before sleep, Clara would shed a few soft tears for infant daughter Catherine, laid to rest at St. Michael's cemetery a fortnight ago, as George comforted her and read from the Bible. Life was good for the well-to-do Barkleys, but still they were impacted by the harsh environment of early Pensacola and afflicted with the full gamut of human emotion. Lest we forget, their daily world lacked much of the creature comfort we take for granted in the 21st Century.

The Barkleys and Yellow Fever. Soon after the Barkleys and Garners made their arrival in Pensacola in 1820, the young city was devastated by yellow fever. In the summer of 1822, as the new Florida Territorial Legislature was meeting in Pensacola, an epidemic broke out, driving the legislative body some fifteen miles north to the country home of Don Manuel Gonzalez. The young town was devastated, and according to contemporaneous records, some three hundred of the town's four hundred American residents perished, including the presiding officer of the territorial legislature Dr. Bronaugh and the US Attorney Harrison. Bronaugh had been staying at the home of previous acting governor George Walton at 137 W. Romana Street, short blocks from the Barkleys. Where were the Barkleys during this medical catastrophe? The records are silent, but it would be reasonable to speculate that they rode out the epidemic by temporary return to New Orleans, as physical flight was the surest way to avoid the contagion. Medical science had not identified Pensacola's prodigious mosquitoes as the carrier of this dread disease, and in fact Andrew Jackson wrote to George Walton of his concerns that rotted fish had introduced the scourge. Common treatments for the disease included eating garlic, tying a tarred rope about the waist, burning bonfires, and covering the mouth with sponges dipped in vinegar. Despite primitive medical knowledge and harsh conditions, and fortunately for the young city, the entire Barkley and Garnier families survived the terrible epidemic of 1822 enabling Barkley's rise to positions of leadership and prominence, and to sire generations of Barkley descendants who still call Pensacola home.

The Duel, "Code Duello." As anachronistic as it sounds today, the European tradition of men settling arguments by duelling was common in territorial Florida. Masked as matters of honor, they sometimes amounted to nothing more than sanctioned murder. There is evidence that Barkley participated in a duel prior to 1834 and came out unscathed, only to be challenged again. On April 2, 1834, George W. Barkley was handed the following letter by John L. Sansone, through an intermediary, John Gonzales.

"Attention George Barkley. Sir you have grossly insulted me this morning, you know. I for satisfaction applied to you the second time which was the same. Now sir, satisfaction I want from the insult I received no other way but this. Choose your mode of fighting from the mouth of a cannon to the point of a pen knife, four days from this time, pick your place and mode also. Give me an answer in a half hour or cawl(sic) yourself a coward and choose your second and I will mine.

Yours respectfully,

John L. Sansone"

In the Barkley era dueling was a common practice among men to settle disputes. George Barkley was challenged to a duel by a disgruntled citizen named Sansone, but fortunately the murderous event never came to pass when the mayor of Pensacola intervened. Many of the historic figures in this book did however face their enemies on the euphemistically named "field of honor."

Duelling was illegal and Barkley responded accordingly. He went immediately to Mayor Charles Evans who had Sansone arrested. Sansone was tried by a jury of his peers, found guilty, and fined $500 with six months on probation. Barkley, who might have been killed, lived on to become a prominent contributor to early Pensacola, clearly demonstrating the folly of the "Code Duello." The duel has gone the way of the dinosaur and many good men have been spared.

The Environment. To affirm the primitive nature of early Pensacola, the record provides us with this diary entry of Bishop Jackson Kemper. Bishop Kemper was in Pensacola to officiate at the consecration of Christ Church.

"Pensacola, Florida, March 2, 1838
Corner of Romana and Palafox Streets"

"The names of the streets at the corner of which I am now staying might almost induce one to suppose that he is in Spain. I have therefore mentioned them above. This town has quite a novel foreign appearance. It contains about 2,200 inhabitants, and is situated on one of the finest bays in the world. The houses have a foreign appearance similar I suppose to those in the South of Europe. It is actually built on a bed of sand, yet the inhabitants make out to have something like gardens. I have seen fig trees as large as apple trees. On Wednesday afternoon I walked through this place and its northern environs. But beyond the city there are two fine springs, covered over with a good shed, (N.B., atop the gentle rise of Spring Street,) and from which many of the people draw water altho the wells in the town are very good...A little rivulet passes near to the springs to which the washerwomen of the town resort; while close to them there is a thick growth of evergreen bushes on which they dry their clothes. I have walked a considerable distance on the shore but could not find a shell or stone. There is nothing but purely white sand."

Bishop Kemper's descriptions of the austerity of colonial Pensacola came eighteen years after the arrival of George W. Barkley and his Garnier inlaws, and at a time when the population had tripled in the aftermath of Spanish rule! One can then put into perspective just how primitive was the military outpost the Barkleys and Garniers found when they arrived in 1820.

Bishop Kemper goes on to report on gulls, pelicans, and bald eagles; on lagoons and bays; on white sands, marshes and ubiquitous pines which still characterize the area. Fortunately some things haven't changed!

To fully appreciate the harshness of the Barkley's early Pensacola environment, one must appreciate the nature of daily life.

Of course there was no electricity, so taken for granted after its introduction...for lighting, heating, cooking, and more. The Barkley House was heated by its several fireplaces, and cooled by bay breezes, if at all. Cooking was done by slaves in the cook house to the rear of the main house, built there to minimize the possibility of fire

On the Barkley menu: Like today, Pensacola was reknowned for seafood, especially oysters. Of course there would have been fresh meats. Though not up to 21st century standards, the Barkley table would have included chicken, pork, occasional beef, and copious quantities of game, including venison, rabbit, turkey, geese, ducks, doves, quail and assorted small birds. These were raised domestically, trapped in the wild, or shot with the muzzle-loading percussion firearms of the day. If the Barkleys followed old European tradition, even Pensacola's herons may have found their way to the table on occasion. Seasonal vegetables and fruits were plentiful due to long growing seasons.

Barkley's thriving store and imports from New Orleans meant that George and Clara likely ate more lavishly than anyone else in Pensacola. Their diet was enhanced with a ready supply of grains, breads, wines, champagnes, and other spirits imported by coastal boat traffic, including Barkley's own. When hauling bricks and lumber to Mobile and New Orleans, return trips to Pensacola would bring wines, fine fabrics, furniture, arms, dried foodstuffs and other amenities back to Pensacola, where over a dozen wharves greeted merchant traffic, and many tall-masted sailing vessels stood out in the bay on anchor. It was a sight to see, under the glaring sun of sub-tropical Florida!

In addition to merchant vessels, in 1839, Reverend Walker Anderson of Christ Church described seeing both American and French squadrons of warships at anchor in the roads between Pensacola proper and the peninsula we now know as Gulf Breeze. Sometimes over a hundred masts pierced the southern sky just offshore.

George Barkley's two ships, the YANKEE and the ALEXANDER OF PENSACOLA, home-ported at his private wharf on Barkley Point, on the north shore of Pensacola Bay just south of today's Barkley House. The harbor of early Pensacola and the roads just offshore were alive with ships of many nations.

Back on land, the small community, measuring about one mile on each dimension, the rutted sand tracks which passed for streets would have accommodated a variety of carriages, wagons, buggies, horses, mules, donkeys, and the ubiquitous foot traffic. It would be generations later when streets began to be paved. Commerce (and everything else!) moved at a snails pace, often bogging down in rutted sugar-white sand, occasionally surfaced with oyster shells. George and Clara Barkley, as befitting their status, traveled by carriage, a fact we know from descriptions of the carriage house associated with the Barkley House at 410 Florida Blanca Street.

As a general rule, homes and commercial buildings in Pensacola tended to be on a smaller and more austere scale than in wealthier French-dominated Mobile and New Orleans. In those cities the wealth of the upperclass was on display with brick mansions furnished in high French fashion at a time when the atmosphere of Pensacola was more like a frontier outpost. In Pensacola, the Barkley House is widely believed to have been the city's earliest masonry residence, though there had been brick military structures and a few brick warehouses for some years.

Barkley era clothing was uniquely ill-suited to colonial Pensacola. Stiff collars and ties for the men, and long dresses underlayed with starched petticoats for the women were the norm, along with hats for both. Woolens (for which there were no dry-cleaning plants) and cottons, which required extensive hand maintenance, were *de riguer*, but must have been frustrating in the heat and humidity of a Pensacola summer. Imported silks were worn by the ladies on special occasions, but Pensacola was more of a working town than a center of *diletantte* society as were the French cities to the west.

The dress styles brought by the Barkleys and Garniers from Europe were ill-suited for the harsh conditions of frontier Florida.

Bishop Kemper, in 1838, describes a curious form of social event; which he describes as a holdover from the Spanish era. *"People in masques and grotesque dresses went about throwing flour at all they met...Mrs. Arin Dallas gave a fancy ball that night."* It may be that Bishop Kemper was not witnessing a Spanish custom at all, but rather, an early Mardi Gras, already established in Mobile and New Orleans. A Spanish colonial custom of the "padgo" did survive in the city, with the men shooting a beribboned fake chicken atop a pole, after which followed a dance and much drinking and merriment. Society may have been odd by today's measure, but partying ranging from dress balls in silks to drunken sailors in street brawls kept the young city lively!

The Barkley House Hosted Historic People and Events of the Day. That the Barkley House was a center of social and political activity during the era of their ownership beginning in 1830 is without question. As a civic and business leader of young Pensacola, George Barkley would have surrounded himself with fellow shapers of the city's destiny, involving himself of necessity in contemporary political issues. It is said by Adelaide Willis, a Barkley descendant, in her book "The Willis Family of Virginia" that at the time he was occupying his home at 410 Florida Blanca Street, George W. Barkley *"was the wealthiest man in Pensacola"* and he would have surely entertained accordingly. As the daughter of a French nobleman and very much imbued with continental panache for such matters, we can be sure that Clara Garnier Barkley was socially at home with dignitaries such as Andrew and Rachel Jackson. We have no record that she actually entertained them, and the present Barkley House had not been built during Jackson's tenure in the city, so far as we know, so we must rely on speculation concerning the nature and extent of their relationship. The leap of faith which connects Barkley to Andrew Jackson is a small one: We have previously noted that while Jackson was in Pensacola in 1821 as acting governor of Florida under authority of President Madison, the Barkleys were among the city's most prominent citizens. The entire community numbered only some 700 total residents. With a large population of residual Spanish, the American population was smaller still, and it's leaders and their families numbered less than 50 while Jackson served as acting governor of the territory. These facts empower the reader to decide the likelihood of a Barkley-Jackson relationship.

The Barkleys, Garniers, and Whiffs of French Politics. Still very much connected to unfolding events in post-Napoleonic France, Clara Garnier Barkley and her father John Garnier would have no doubt had passionate conversation in the Barkley House about events on the continent. Over dinner prepared in the home's summer kitchen at the rear of the present structure, perhaps indulging in a fine French wine, it is likely that topics at the Barkley table included the simmering aftermath of the French Revolution, memories of Napoleon's First Empire, the harsh reign of King Charles X, and the continuing struggles of the French to attain the coveted political stability that had been brought about more effectively in America by the Revolution. The French revolution had wrought more instability, while the American revolution, buttressed by that marvel of political wisdom, the US Constitution, had brought stability and prosperity. While the Barkleys and Garniers struggled to establish themselves in Pensacola, France at that time was still shaken and reeling with convoluted politics, the aftermath of the Napoleonic Wars, and shattered dreams of empire. There were endless reorganizations of governments, intrigues to restore the French monarchy, the despotic reign of Charles X, hostilities between the Bourbons and Burgundians, the "White Terror" and more. As French politics lurched from monarchy to consulate to empire to republic to empire and back again, the well connected Garnier family, now in exile and seeking refuge in Florida, longed for the restoration of a French political regime sympathetic to the return of their titles, lands, status and most especially their confiscated fortunes.

It is certain that George Barkley's Garnier in-laws shared these political yearnings with none other than Prince Achille Murat, the exiled eccentric nephew of Napoleon who practiced law in New Orleans with Clara Garnier Barkley's brother, Charles Garnier. Records of the relationship between Pensacola's Garniers and the exiled Prince are scant, due to their status as exiles, quite possibly with a price on their heads during the era of Charles X. Despite the scarcity of detailed records, we can, with snippets of documentation and connecting facts with informed conjecture, speculate about the nature and extent of the connection between the Barkleys, Garniers, Murats, and the House of Napoleon. More on this tale later.

The Barkley House Hosts Other Fateful Discussions. In addition to French politics, as the 19th Century wore on, we would doubtless also find resounding within the walls of the Barkley House the vexing slavery question. As slave owners and traders the Barkley family would doubtless be torn between the moral issues and the practical demands of life in America's southern frontier, which was harsh beyond comprehension as we reflect on it from our air conditioned, prosperous 21st Century vantage point. Resolution of the slavery issue would not come, of course, until the Civil War and the Emancipation Proclamation; events George Barkley would not live to see.

Without question another hot topic in the drawing room of the Barkley House would have been lively discussion of Florida statehood. No doubt the ambitious merchant Barkley was a proponent of statehood to protect and further his economic interests. Surely the Barkley House rang with festive celebration when Florida became the 27th state of the union on March 3, 1845. Barkley's gamble 25 years earlier had paid off, and he now enjoyed the stability, prosperity and freedoms afforded by American rule and now by statehood. Though today, with the hindsight of our knowledge of America's westward migration we no longer perceive it as such, Pensacola was perceived as one of the western cities of the US at the time of statehood.

With his banking and merchant interests, no doubt George Barkley's guests would have discussed trade, relationships with the Spanish, British, and French contenders for influence along the coast, the burgeoning fortification of the port city (this era heralded the start of construction of the three harbor defenses, Forts Pickens, McRee, and Barrancas), the Seminole Indian Wars, the political future of the fledgling United States…along with such immediately practical issues as transport of goods to markets, development of Pensacola and it's infrastructure, the economy of the West Florida Territory, and means to develop and exploit the region's rich resources, especially it's seemingly endless production of timber.

A Social Center of Pensacola. One of Pensacola's finest residences, the Barkley House hosted Pensacola's top social and political circles, as well as some of the sophisticated elites of New Orleans and Mobile. No doubt the Barkley House's halls rang with music and laughter, as well serious business talk and political debate. Not far away, at the corner of Palafox and Romana Streets, lived Barkley colleague George Walton II, son of a signer of the Declaration of Independence, Georgia governor George Walton I and his wife Dorothy. Having arrived in Pensacola as Secretary to Andrew Jackson, George Walton II later served as acting governor of the Florida Territory before President Monroe's appointment of William P. DuVal as permanent governor. In the small close-knit environment of early Pensacola, the Walton's young and accomplished daughter Octavia, age 10 upon their arrival in Pensacola, doubtless was a childhood friend of the Barkley children. The story of this Barkley associate is amazing. Because she spoke fluent Spanish and four other languages in childhood, her father enlisted her to translate documents during the transition from Spanish colony to U.S. Territory. The consummate diplomat even in her youth, it is also documented that Seminole Chief Namantha called her "The White Dove of Peace" because she could cajole her father into granting the Indians permits to travel. They taught her, she says, the Seminole word for Florida; "Tallahassee" … "beautiful land", and family lore of the Waltons holds that when it came time to name the new capital, Octavia's father asked of her what she thought, to which she gave the fateful and historic answer…"Tallahassee."

At age 14, this young neighbor of the Barkleys traveled to Mobile at the request of her mother, Dorothy Camber Walton, to honor the esteemed Marquis de Lafayette. Even at that tender age the brilliant and beautiful Pensacolian was dazzling, and spoke, in perfect French, at length with the venerable Lafayette about her home by the bay.

Octavia lived near the Barkleys for fifteen years, and describes that "*I lived a merry life in Pensacola enjoying the dances and parties that so shocked Rachel Jackson. In 1835, when I was 25, my parents moved to Mobile where my home was open to stimulating people from all walks of life.*"

Octavia Celestia Valentine Walton was the accomplished daughter of territorial governor George Walton II and was a contemporary, neighbor, and friend of the Barkley children. Octavia Walton married Dr. Henry S. LeVert and was a renowned intellectual and socialite of the Gulf coast. Her status and fame was such that this portrait is by the well known artist Thomas Sully, renowned for his portraits of John Quincy Adams, Queen Victoria, the Marquis de Lafayette, and other figures of international prominence. Through this close neighbor and colleague of George and Clara Barkley, any number of famous persons may have been entertained at the Barkley House since it was the finest residence in Pensacola and was located very near the Walton residence.

"Miss Walton of Florida" by Thomas Sully, Historic Mobile Preservation Society, Oakleigh Museum Collection.

In Mobile she would be celebrated as the illustrious Madame Octavia Walton LeVert, herself the very epicenter of society on the Gulf Coast from her marital home on Government Street. Octavia's father, late of Pensacola as Andrew Jackson's appointee as acting governor, served at that time as Mobile's mayor. Pensacola-educated Octavia Walton married Dr. Henry Le Vert, son of Dr. Claude Le Vert, a surgeon with Rochambeau's fleet during the American Revolution and they lived in an elegant brick mansion at 151 Government Street. Family friend and distinguished author Washington

When Barkley neighbor, the sophisticated Octavia Walton, moved to Mobile with her parents in 1835 she married Dr. Henry LeVert. Pictured above is the LeVert mansion at 151 Government Street in Mobile, Alabama. While the splendid home has been torn down to accommodate a contemporary courthouse, her husband's medical office at 153 Government Street remains. Her father, late of Pensacola, became mayor of Mobile after his tenure as territorial governor of Florida. The well-connected Madame LeVert, early compatriot of the Pensacola Barkley's, was revered; only partly tongue in cheek, as the "countess of Mobile".

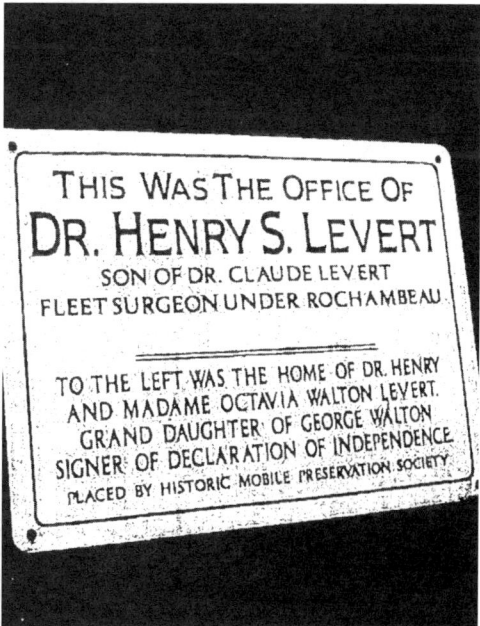

THIS WAS THE OFFICE OF
DR. HENRY S. LEVERT
SON OF DR. CLAUDE LEVERT
FLEET SURGEON UNDER ROCHAMBEAU

TO THE LEFT WAS THE HOME OF DR. HENRY AND MADAME OCTAVIA WALTON LEVERT. GRAND DAUGHTER OF GEORGE WALTON SIGNER OF DECLARATION OF INDEPENDENCE PLACED BY HISTORIC MOBILE PRESERVATION SOCIETY

Irving is quoted as saying of Octavia Walton Le Vert, that "*a century produces only one such woman.*", and the cultural and literary accomplishments of this childhood friend of the Barkley children were legendary, while her social graces without peer. As well as Washington Irving, she describes making the acquaintance of Henry Clay, Henry Wordsworth Longfellow, Edwin Booth, Elizabeth Barrett Browning, Lord Byron, Napoleon III, the Marquis de Lafayette, General P.G.T. Beauregard, Queen Victoria, and an admiring Edgar Allen Poe, who wrote her moody love poems.

To Octavia

When wit, and wine, and friends have met
And laughter crowns the festive hour
In vain I struggle to forget
Still does my heart confess thy power
And fondly turn to thee!

But Octavia, do not strive to rob
My heart of all that soothes its pain
The mournful hope that every throb
Will make it break for thee!

May the 1st 1827

Edgar Allen Poe

Poe's, "To Octavia" appears in his collection <u>Tamerlane and Other Poems</u>, published in 1827 while she lived in Pensacola.

Apparently Octavia had this mesmerizing effect on many young men. A young officer at the recently established Pensacola Navy Yard was so smitten with Octavia that he wrote effusively that *"Nothing could exceed the brilliancy of her eyes or the fascination of her smile. Dazzlingly beautiful, wherever she moves there is light in her path...She possesses in the highest perfection all the tender, retiring attributes of women. Being almost nature's masterpiece, it is almost impossible to wish her different."* That smitten young officer was Franklin Buchanan, later to rise to admiral, thence to resign to serve the confederacy, thereafter to rise to become one of the US Navy's most distinguished sons, and to found the US Naval Academy.

No less than the Marquis de Lafayette had predicted a "brilliant future" for this childhood friend of the Barkleys and he would not have been disappointed. Octavia Walton LeVert was the original "Iron Magnolia" whose intelligence, charm, social graces, and political acumen are legendary even to this day. Alas, in attempting to reconcile north and south during the Civil War, Octavia, childhood friend of the Barkleys and celebrated as the "Belle of the Nation", was branded a "turncoat" and forced to flee her beloved Gulf Coast forever.

As a close family friend of George and Sarah Walton, who lived near the Barkleys, it is surely possible that distinguished author Washington Irving and the Barkleys were acquainted through their mutual link to the Waltons. Given the Barkley's reputation for cosmopolitan hospitality and the small, compact nature of early Pensacola society, it is at least possible that during a visit to the Walton's Washington Irving may have been entertained at the Barkley House. While the record is silent, it is surely a distinct...and intriguing... possibility.

George Barkley may well have been involved too in a duel in which his neighbor George Walton; targeted by vicious gossip, engaged. On May 27, 1829 Walton challenged one of his critics, Dr. McMahon, to the so-called "field of honor." The duel was fought on Santa Rosa Island, and Walton was severely wounded by his opponent's second shot. His seconds, fearing for his life, halted the duel, but then had to offer to the Pensacola *Gazette* an explanation for why the duel was discontinued. Was Walton's neighbor and friend George Barkley, among them? We may never know, but who more likely than a neighbor and trusted colleague? ... leaving us with yet another tantalizingly incomplete vignette.

The French Connection; Garnier, Le Vert, Murat and More...a Backdrop of Continental Elegance for The Barkley House. The earlier owner of the land upon which the Barkley House stands, Charles Garnier (Clara's brother) doubtless brought the news of the day to Pensacola from

New Orleans, along with the French sophistication of that city's social life. Though the physical environment of the Florida frontier was spartan by comparison to the cities of the east, back in Europe, and even in neighboring Mobile and New Orleans, the Barkley's social graces would have rivalled any known in early 19th Century America, composed of a cultured, multi-lingual cast of characters. Together with other resettled French who visited from Francophile Mobile and New Orleans, the halls of the Barkley House were accustomed to the melodious *lingua franca*. French was the first language of both Madame Clara Garnier Barkley and the other Garniers. Of course Spanish was much spoken in Pensacola, and would likely have been interspersed in conversation with neighbors and colleagues such as the De la Ruas. London-born George Barkley's "Kings English", perhaps tinged with a slight Scottish brogue, no doubt also prevailed within the halls of the stately Barkley House. Fluency in several languages was considered a hallmark of an educated person, and as a practical matter, was much needed in multi-cultural Pensacola.

We have earlier noted the sophistication of their friends the Waltons, and the peak level of social graces they affected, and they were but one such example of Barkley House's multi-lingual guests. Young Pensacola may have been austere, but it's society was cosmopolitan indeed, reflecting the rich gumbo of cultures which characterized the Gulf Coast.

More on the Family of the Barkley House's First Lady; the Garnier Family. George Barkley the English merchant, and his wife Clara Louise Garnier Barkley, the French aristocrat, were clearly among Pensacola's leaders and most prominent citizens. Clara Garnier Barkley had been born ca. 1800 in Bordeaux, France, the daughter of French aristocrat John (Jean) Garnier, Sr. This elder Garnier, John (Jean) Sr. had been born, presumably in Bordeaux, in about 1765, and there married a lady about 1790, by whom he had at least four children; John, Jr., Clara Louise, Charles, and Rosa. There is well-informed speculation that his French-born wife's name was Adeline, as Garnier tradition strongly enforces the continuance of names within the family. He had a daughter in Pensacola whom he named Adeline in her honor, and both Clara and John, Jr. had daughters to whom the name Adeline was given.

Though some believe that Pensacola's John Garnier, Senior fled to America as a Huguenot to escape religious persecution, it is even more likely that, as a member of the aristocracy, he sought safety from political persecution or even execution in the era of bloodshed wrought by out-of-control political retribution in France. The timing would be right for a timely escape from the bloody regime of Charles X.

The Huguenot migrations had, after all, largely occurred over a century before John Garnier made his way to Pensacola. It is more likely that he was both a French Protestant and political refugee, in self-imposed exile to avert the violence which was visited on aristocratic French families in the early 1800's. In support of his Huguenot Protestant church loyalties, we note that nowhere in the record is there mention of Catholicism with regard to John Garnier or any member of his family, and we know that his daughter Clara married Protestant Barkley without any discussion of marrying outside the faith. John Garnier himself married at least twice. We are content with the notion of Garnier as a political refugee, and shall develop a theory of Garnier's possible connections to the Bonaparte empire and subsequent developments in post Napoleonic France.

The Garniers in France. The Garnier's were an aristocratic family of high station; so distinguished that their family's name adorns the famous Paris Opera House, the Palais de Garnier. In building this monument to the arts, Emperor Napoleon III selected a member of the Garnier family, for whom the lavish edifice is named.

Even today the Garnier name is highly respected in Paris.

L'Opéra de Paris

Napoleon III chose a member of the Garnier family, Charles, to design his opus project; the famed Paris Opera House, still known as the Palais de Garnier.

Emperor Napoleon III is remembered largely for the rebuilding of Paris under Baron Hausmann. Large sections of the city were razed and the old convoluted streets were replaced with many broad avenues, with the intent of allowing cannon and cavalry to be used easily within the city.

So associated with French aristocracy was the Garnier name that in the tumult of the times they appear to have been persecuted and driven from power. Vengeful mobs sometimes sought the heads of those who had supported out-of-power leaders, and the Garniers were probably caught up as victims of the hysteria. We know with a certainty that their titles, lands, and most of their fortunes were confiscated. In this bloody and hostile atmosphere, the Garniers were likely on the short list for persecution, if not execution. In the Library of Congress is a genealogical history of the distinguished family of Garnier of France, many of whom, it is stated, left their homeland for political reasons, and we posit that John Garnier and his family were among those who fled, seeking safety in America. It is assumed that the family escaped with some of their fortunes intact for in 1817 John Garnier Jr. bought a lavish home on Saint Peter's Street in New Orleans after the Garnier migration there. It would be highly unlikely that he would have had time to accrue sufficient money after arrival…thus making the case for arrival in New Orleans with at least some Garnier assets whisked from France. At the same time his brother Charles Garnier was spending freely as a real estate speculator in Pensacola, and one must assume, as with brother John, that Charles' money had French origins. Both Garnier brothers and their wives were active in the slave trade, also suggesting a measure of wealth which must have surely been secreted out of France on their flight to America.

John Garnier, Sr. Arrives in America. Amid the turmoil of early 19th Century France, John Garnier, Sr. and his children, escaped to the fledgling United States about 1815, first to Wilmington, NC, then known as New Liverpool. We don't know how long he stayed there, but it was long enough to marry an American wife, Ann, whose last name remains a mystery.

No doubt in response to the magnet of French culture and perhaps in hopes of a political alliance which would facilitate the recoupment of his fortunes in France, it was then onward to New Orleans and finally Pensacola for the Garniers. It is not known if his first wife (probably Adeline, supra) became a victim of the bloodletting that swept France, but it is known that when Jean (John) Garnier arrived in the US, he arrived as a widower, with his family in tow; John, Jr., Clara Louise, Charles, and Rosa. We know very little of John Garnier's American wife Ann. From her stone in Pensacola's St. Michaels Cemetery we find that she was born in 1790, and we know that she bore him a daughter, Adeline.

Together, the Garnier family settled next in New Orleans, comfortable in the quintessentially French atmosphere of the city, and in the company of others whose lives in France had been turned upside down in the turmoil of the post-Napoleonic power vacuum. Napoleonic dreams died hard in New Orleans, and the city's venerable Napoleon House, planned to be Napoleon's home should he escape his exile, testifies to rumored plans for the exiled dictator to escape to a new future in America. Fanciful dreams perhaps, for history of course shows us now that such grandiose plans were not to be, snuffed out by Napoleon's death in exile on St. Helena on May 5, 1821.

In this atmosphere of French influence along the Gulf coast, in about 1820 we find that the French Garnier family left New Orleans for unknown reasons, making its way to the capital of the Spanish West Florida; Pensacola. There are unproven hints that they may have stopped briefly in Mississippi, for the Mississippi coast was French too, and there is a record of the elder John Garnier's insolvency there; puzzling in light of the evident wealth of his New Orleans sons. Probably John Garnier's move onward to Pensacola anticipated the imminent end of the Spanish occupation and the opportunities for wealth that change might bring. There was growing realization too that America's recent Louisiana Purchase foretold huge wealth and potential.

Later in Pensacola, John Garnier and his American-born wife, Ann would have another daughter born about 1830, hauntingly named, it is believed, for John Garnier's first wife Adeline who had perhaps fallen to political reprisals in France. The name Adeline lives on in subsequent generations of Garniers in America, honoring the first wife of John Garnier who perished before he immigrated to America. This Pensacola-born Adeline Garnier married widower Josiah Shippey, and they were active in both Christ Church and in the establishment of the new Episcopal Church, Saint Johns, in Warrington.

John's daughter, Clara Louise Garnier, by his first wife in France would marry George W. Barkley and become first lady of Pensacola's revered Barkley House. His other French-born daughter Rosa married Pensacola apothecary John O. Smith. Son Charles became a prominent businessman and attorney in New Orleans in partnership with the nephew of Napoleon, while son John, Jr. enjoyed success in New Orleans as a cotton and slave trader and supplier to plantations along the river.

Much of the Garnier history in this country is conjectural as they lived discreet and unremarkable lives, not wishing to call attention to themselves for fear of potential retribution from France. Because they chose low-profile lives there are few documents of their lives on the Gulf Coast, and we are left with tantalizing tidbits of evidence from which to try to recreate the fabric of their lives in the Florida and Louisiana Territories. This requires then a good bit of speculation about events and family connections which make logical sense, but which cannot be proved beyond all doubt from the skimpy available evidence. It is for us to assign meaning to the few facts we <u>do</u> have.

The Struggles of John Garnier. We do know that in Pensacola, in unaccustomed austerity, displaced French aristocrat John Garnier, Sr. was first appointed to several government-related jobs. The Territorial Papers of the United States for the Territory of Florida document that in 1822, John Garnier served as Justice of Escambia County, Justice of the Peace, and

Justice of the Quorum. The same record also contains interesting personal correspondence between Garnier and John Quincy Adams, then US Secretary of State. According to *"Documents Reflecting the Records of Pensacola's Elected Officials"*, an unpublished manuscript by the City Clerk's Office of Pensacola, John Garnier also served one term in 1828 as an alderman of the young city. Despite such appointments, Garnier ... accustomed to the life of privilege of a French aristocrat ... found adaptation to the primitive world of the heat, sand streets, and lack of continental amenities of Pensacola a constant struggle and disappointment. He clearly was a victim of what we would label today as "culture shock"! Despite extensive backing from his son Charles, and from his son-in-law George W. Barkley, John Garnier never put together the magic elixir of success. He had a plantation near Valparaiso, Florida, but was not financially able to buy slaves with which to work it. Apparently he rented seven slaves for $580 a year, but their master died and they returned with their mistress to Virginia. Garnier lost his plantation in a land dispute, after review of the matter by US Secretary of State John Adams. He and his wife Ann leased the City Hotel in Pensacola for several years intending a profit, but it too failed. He then sold timber, sold coffee, and tried to become the model of the American entrepreneur in so many ways, yet lived an unfulfilled life amid the heat and sand of his adopted home. Today he might feel partially vindicated that Florida maps disclose near Eglin AFB a tributary of Choctawhatchee Bay named Garnier Bayou, and the small village of Garnier, aka, Cairo, on highway 85 between Fort Walton and Valparaiso. Both memorialize John Garnier's plantation in that vicinity.

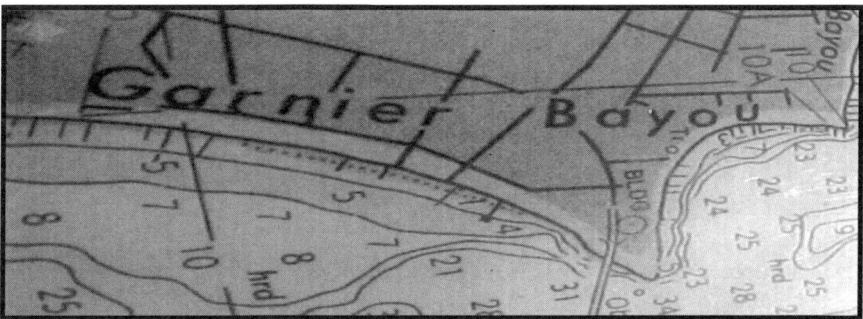

Clara Louise Garnier Barkley's father John was accustomed to a life of privilege and status in France. A victim of "culture shock", John Garnier failed in his efforts to become a successful entrepreneur in his new life in exile on the Gulf Coast. One especially poignant reminder of the plantation he had near Valparaiso, Florida, is Garnier Bayou, a tributary of Choctawhatchee Bay.

Simultaneously with the elder Garnier's attempts to carve out a new life in Pensacola, the political turmoil which had displaced him from his native France raged on. In the internecine power struggles between Bourbons and Burgundians countless Frenchmen lost their heads to the guillotine rendering life in France even more precarious. In a continuation of over eight centuries of warfare the seemingly intractable conflict between French and British dominated Atlantic Europe. We do not know the exact circumstance which drove Garnier from his homeland, but we do know that at some personal peril, the exiled John Garnier, like many French exiles along the Gulf Coast, held controversial political dreams which were not to be. The politics that sent the Garniers into exile in Pensacola and New Orleans were to have lasting impact, impact which resonated within the walls of Pensacola's Barkley House and it's French in-laws. The Garniers had close connections to the House of Bonaparte and the passions which went with it. And Clara Garnier, we shall remember, became Mrs. George Barkley, tying George Barkely's fate to the convulsions of French politics.

Charles Garnier, Brother of Pensacola's Clara Garnier Barkley, Practiced Law with the Nephew of Napoleon. Two of John Garnier's sons, John Jr. and Charles L. Garnier, a Pensacola land speculator well known in public circles, continued to reside in New Orleans when his father and sisters moved to Pensacola. In the old-world atmosphere of New Orleans, they fell in easily with a sophisticated, if transplanted, French society. There the Garnier sons found a congenial atmosphere among displaced French of all political stripes, each jockeying for advantage in both the new world of "Nouvelle Orleans" while hedging their bets at home in France. There was French culture, French language, French law, and French foods still famous in New Orleans today suited them just fine! In those heady days, with Napoleon in exile, in New Orleans a way was being prepared for the Emperor's escape to New Orleans. The famed Napoleon House, which was to be his home, still stands at at 500 Chartres Street, now open to the public as a bar and restaurant.

Another likely historic connection of Clara Garnier Barkley's brothers was to famed naturalist, John James Audobon. Among Audobon's extensive diaries is a near-tragic description of losing a folio of his drawings, now world-famous, of the waterfowl of the Mississippi River basin. John Garnier, Jr. was prominent in New Orleans as a "commission merchant"…plying the trade of shipping cotton to market from upriver plantations in return for supplying their needs for the lavish plantation lifestyle. Garnier was evidently a frequent figure in river life when Audobon was traveling the lower Mississippi by keel-boat sketching. Audobon describes his angst at misplacing a folio of priceless sketches, but then in a later passage of his diaries expresses thanks for the safe return of his drawings. *Through the kindness of Mr. Garnier, I received it on the 5th of April. So very generous had been the finder of it, that when I carefully examined the drawings in succession, I found them all present and uninjured, save one, which had probably been kept by way of commission.* Was this our Pensacola-connected "Mr Garnier"? Audubon is silent as to first name of the benefactor who returned his drawings, but one could well ask "How many Garniers were about on the lower Mississippi in the winter of 1820?" Maybe it was Clara Garnier Barkley's brother in law; maybe not. But it is at least possible that the world might not know today the wondrous works of John James Audubon but for the honesty and kindness of this Barkley family in law.

In New Orleans, Charles Garnier, brother of Clara Garnier Barkley, practiced the familiar law of France in the only US venue which still, to this day, honors and practices the Napoleonic Code. Like his father John in Pensacola, Charles Garnier and his brother John, Jr. also maintained close contact with refugees seeking the overthrow of Charles X, among whom was Napoleon's nephew, the eccentric Achille Murat, Crown Prince of Naples and the Two Sicilies. Achille was the son of Marshal of France and King of the Napoleonic Kingdom of Naples, Joachim Murat and his wife Caroline Bonaparte, the eldest sister of Napoleon. Blueblooded Bonaparte credentials indeed!

Though the young Bonapartist nobleman Achille Murat was something of an eccentric tumbleweed who drifted from venture to venture along the Gulf Coast, he had a keen mind, knew the Napoleonic Codes by which the Louisiana Territory governed itself, and was a shrewd political operator. It was a natural marriage of interests that led Charles Garnier and Prince Achille Murat to become partners in New Orleans law practice located in Exchange Alley and a few unrelated business ventures. Murat lived in a fine mansion at 919 Esplanade Street during the days of his law practice with George Barkley's brother in law, dabbled with a cotton plantation known as Magnolia Mound near Baton Rouge, and invested in railroad enterprises in Texas and a canal venture near Appalachicola. His hot temper, lack of business skills, and perhaps his fondness for alcohol caused the collapse of all.

Charles Louis Napoleon Achille Murat, crown prince of Naples, son of Napoleon's sister Caroline and her husband King Joachim Murat was a political colleague and law partner of George Barkley's in-laws, the Garniers. Raised in splendor and royalty in Paris' Elysee Palace, Murat is linked to the Barkley House through both the Garnier and Willis families. His wife was the daughter of a Barkley colleague and business associate, Colonel Byrd Charles Willis.

Though unrelated by blood, the family of Clara Garnier Barkley was surely allied in both business and passionate French politics with the exiled nobleman Murat, whose father had given Napoleon his greatest victories; the Battle of the Pyramids in Egypt, Austerlitz, Jena, Borodino and others. Though known for his eccentricities, Achille Murat was a political wild card to be reckoned with. European rulers who saw in him a potential resurgence of Napoleonic power on the continent were quite happy that he was safely ensconced in rustic northwest Florida and New Orleans, posing no immediate threat.

The father of Barkley House visitor Prince Achille Murat was Napoleon's greatest cavalry commander, King Joachim Murat. Napoleon made him a Marshal of the Empire, Grand Duke of Berg and Cleves, and king of Naples, comprising the southern third of Italy. The battlefield exploits of this father of a Barkley House guest were legendary. He was one of the small cadre of the most influential leaders during Napoleon's rise to power and expansion into empire and wrote to his son and Pensacola daughter in law of events on the continent. King Murat was put to death by firing squad for attempting to unify Italy under his leadership during the last gasp of Napoleon's First Empire. His son married Catherine Willis, the daughter of Pensacola brick maker Colonel Byrd Charles Willis and a close Barkley associate.

As law partners and political cronies, Clara Barkley's brother-in-law Charles Garnier and the deposed, exiled Prince Murat lobbied ceaselessly for Bonapartist causes. Their motives were no doubt economic as well as idealistic, for if successful, the French fortunes of the Garnier and Murat families may have been restored along with their various titles and privileged status in social and government circles.

Garnier's Connections With Charles Louis Napoleon Achille Murat, Crown Prince of Naples. Achille Murat was a fascinating character of the early Florida frontier. Bear with us, for the historic connection to the Garniers of Pensacola and to the Barkley House shall become apparent.

Caroline Bonaparte, sister of Napoleon, and queen of Naples. Her son, who almost certainly spent considerable time at Pensacola's Barkley House, was a law partner of Barkley in-law Charles Garnier, and married the daughter of another Barkley protegé Colonel Byrd Charles Willis.

As the eldest son of Napoleon's sister Caroline, and King (of the Napoleonic Kingdom of Naples; the lower third of Italy) Joachim Murat. Young Achille was raised in imperial splendor in his parents great estate at Neuilly, and later in the sumptuous Elysee Palace in Paris. Today, the Elysee Palace, boyhood home of the maverick Achille Murat of frontier Florida, is France's "White House", home to the President of France. During the heyday of the First Empire, Emperor Napoleon I rewarded his father's loyalty and military prowess by making Joachim Murat first the Grand Duke of Berg and Cleves, and later the King of Naples. The Napoleonic Kingdom of Naples encompassed a great deal more than the city of that name, consisting of roughly the southern third of Italy. Under this Napoleonic patronage, young Achille, as King Murat's eldest son, was awarded the status of Crown Prince of Naples. He was a special favorite of his Uncle Napoleon, and could scarcely be ignored when the spoils of war were being passed around!

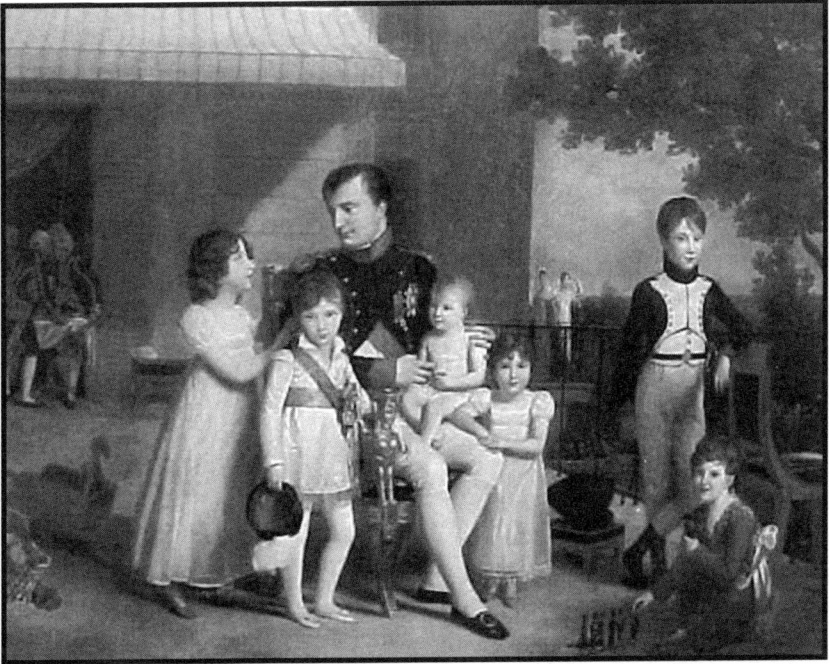

The young boy in uniform in this picture is Prince Achille Murat at age 12 with his uncle, the Emperor Napoleon I. After the death of his father by firing squad, Murat moved to the Florida Territory and practiced law in New Orleans with Clara Garnier Barkley's brother, Charles Garnier.

The brilliant, eccentric Prince Murat married the daughter of George Barkley's business associate Byrd Charles Willis. These and other historic records conclusively link Prince Murat to the Pensacola Barkleys.

Just as John Garnier escaped to Pensacola, Achille Murat, with his mother and siblings had also been forced to flee the turmoil which ended the Napoleonic Empire and ended the life of his father, King Joachim as well. His mother Caroline Bonaparte Murat retreated with her oldest son Achille and her other children to Frohsdorf Castle in Austria, where she, deposed queen of Naples, lived under the assumed title, Countess of Lipona, and under the protections and close scrutiny of Metternich's government.

49

Barkley cohort Prince Murat was raised in imperial splendor in Paris' Elysee Palace (now the residence of the President of France) and just prior to immigrating to the United States, Prince Achille Murat lived in exile in Austria's Frohsdorf Castle from age 14 - 21. Incongruously the eccentric son of royalty, Achille Murat, would later live in a log cabin outside Tallahassee, where he held minor positions in government and wrote profusely about American style democracy. There he wistfully named his plantation "Lipona", an anagram for "Napoli", the lost kingdom of the Murat's. At that time his mother, Napoleon's sister Caroline, still in exile in Austria, styled herself the Countess of Lipona. Murat was affiliated in business and politics with the Garnier family of Pensacola and married the daughter of a Pensacola brick maker.

Elysee Palace

Frohsdorf Castle

Seven years later, upon attainment of his majority, her ambitious and headstrong son Achille, sensed no future in the anti-Bonapartist sentiment of Europe, and chafing for freedom and self-expression, fled to the safety of the United States, by way of a brief stop in Hamburg, Germany.

Two Barkley House visitors, Prince Achille Murat and Colonel Byrd Charles Willis are known to have been colleagues of Joseph Bonaparte (pictured at left) and to have visited him at his estate-in-exile, "Point Breeze," in New Jersey. Joseph Bonaparte was Napoleon's brother and former King of Spain.

After visiting "Point Breeze", the New Jersey estate of Napoleon's brother Joseph, ex-king of Spain, (where Joseph led a lavish lifestyle supported in part by more than $20 million Francs in the form of the royal diamonds of Spain with which he had absconded while serving as Napoleon's puppet king there.), Achille Murat settled briefly in Washington, DC, where he befriended the Florida Territory's representative, Pensacola attorney and hero of the Seminole wars, Richard Keith Call. Call intrigued the impressionable Murat with tales of the opportunities on the Florida frontier. However ill-prepared the young nobleman Murat was for the course lifestyle of the southern frontier, Napoleon's impetuous nephew Prince Achille Murat, at the urgings of both Pensacola attorney Richard Keith Call and his French friend, the Marquis de Lafayette, moved to the Florida Territory. Murat transited through Charleston, which he pronounced the most amenable city he had ever visited, then traveled by the sloop RAPID to Saint Augustine, where he had purchased a small house on St. George Street and bought a 1200 acre estate on the Matanzas River which he wistfully named "Parthenope"; the ancient name for Naples, a brooding reflection of his late father's lost kingdom of Naples. Murat's little house still stands in Saint Augustine.

Prince Achille Murat lived first in St. Augustine in this house which still stands on St. George Street then owned a plantation on the Matanzas River named "Parthenope." He was a colleague of the Garnier family of the Barkley House (George Barkley's wife was Clara Garnier) and in-law of Barkley protegé Byrd Charles Willis.

In 1824 he moved to Tallahassee at a time when the sparsely settled crossroads was selected as capital of the Florida Territory. Just outside Tallahassee, Prince Murat purchased a plantation with which he hoped to recoup the fortunes lost by the family in Europe, and bide his time until favorable political conditions in Europe. There, at his plantation "Lipona", he became an astute observer and chronicler of the American political system, writing several books while he schemed for the overthrow of the Bourbon government in France and restoration of his titles and fortunes on the continent. Murat was an approximate contemporary of his better known colleague and political writer, Alexis de Toqueville, and like de Toqueville was fascinated by grass-roots democracy as it was practiced in America. Especially poignant is the line from his <u>America</u> <u>and</u> <u>the</u> <u>Americans</u>, published in 1851 after his death, in which the transplanted nobleman writes *"I came to America, poor, friendless, and an exile, and have here found a home and country which Europe refused me."*

Prince Achille Murat was motivated to settle on the Florida frontier by both the Marquis de Lafayette and by Pensacola lawyer Richard Keith Call who served as governor and territorial representative to Congress.

Marquis de Lafayette

Richard Keith Call

The name of Murat's Tallahassee plantation, "Lipona", was an anagram, eg, created by transposing the syllabic order of "Napoli"...Naples ... and was in fact a nostalgic nod to the Murat's lost kingdom, as well as a tribute to his mother Caroline Bonaparte Murat, who after her husband's death by firing squad assumed the title "Countess of Lipona" and lived out her days under the protection of Prince Metternich of Austria at the Castle Frohsdorf.

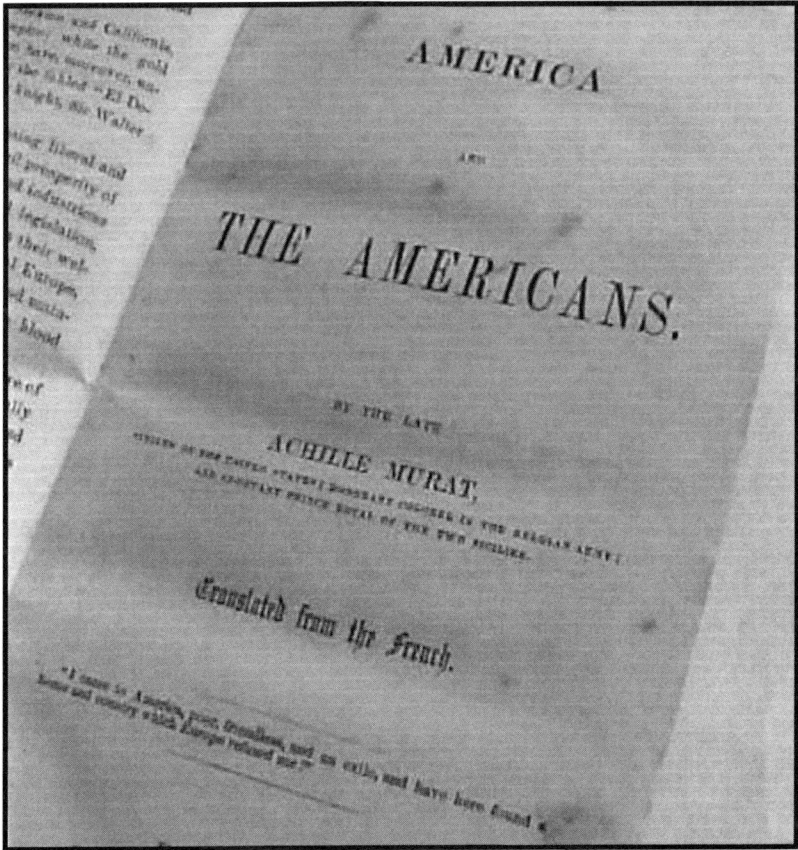

AMERICA

AND

THE AMERICANS.

BY THE LATE

ACHILLE MURAT,

CITIZEN OF THE UNITED STATES; HONORARY COLONEL IN THE BELGIAN ARMY;
AND CI-DEVANT PRINCE ROYAL OF THE TWO SICILIES.

Translated from the French.

One of Achille Murat's treatises on American style democracy, in the vein of his colleague and countryman Alexis de Toqueville. His works, it is said, are still the manual of the democrats of western Europe. Despite his richly fertile mind and connection to royalty, Achille Murat suffered fits of epilepsy and depression, and had a reputation as an unpredictable, if intellectual, maverick. He never recovered from his father Joachim's death by firing squad as the empire of Napoleon collapsed. Achille died in Wacissa, Florida, without ever realizing his dream of recapturing his family's fortunes and titles in France.

During the final collapse of the Napoleonic empire, Achille Murat's father, ex-King Joachim faced a firing squad at Pizzo, Italy in 1815. Seeking personal advantage in the final days of Napoleon's empire, Joachim and Caroline, the Emperor's own sister, played and lost the game of double-cross by attempting to create with Prince Metternich of Austria an alliance which would oppose Napoleon's remaining forces and establish Joachim Murat as king of a united Italy. The scheme, born of betrayal of his patron Napoleon I, collapsed and King Joachim, father of Barkley colleague Achille Murat, was captured and shot. At his execution he refused a blindfold and directed his own firing squad, imploring them as a final act of his vanity not to shoot him in the face. But back from Italy to frontier Florida and his son, the mercurial Achille, child of royalty and the Elysee Palace, now a cracker planter.

A social sensation in the backwoods Florida territory near the new capital of Tallahassee, Achille Murat became an avid naturalist, was appointed a colonel in the Florida militia, named postmaster of Lipona, became a county judge, and served as translator for he courts of central Florida, since he was fluent in seven languages.

Before long, the young exiled prince met the lovely 23-year-old widow Catherine Daingerfield Willis Gray, affectionately known as Kate, at a picnic at the ruins of Tallahassee's old Spanish Fort San Luis. Though her chief asset was her beauty, it didn't hurt that she was the great grandniece of George Washington, a genealogical connection that fascinated Murat and frontier Floridians alike. At Fort San Luis on that fateful day, Achille Murat snatched one of Kate's slippers and drank wine from it, attempting to gain her attention.

This drawing by John Rae originally appeared in "A Prince in Their Midst: The Adventuresome Life of Achille Murat on the American Frontier", by A.J. Hanna, published in 1946 by The University of Oklahoma Press. The author gratefully acknowledges the permission of the University of Oklahoma Press to reproduce this image of the fanciful Tallahassee meeting of Caroline Bonaparte's son, Prince Achille Murat, and Catherine Willis, whose family later resided in Pensacola. From this meeting arose the intermarriage of the families of Napoleon Bonaparte and George Washington.

Kate, a Virginia native, had come south with her father, Col. Byrd Charles Willis, and other family members when his fortunes collapsed.

When Achille Murat began courting Kate, tongues wagged as gossip about the romance between the Houses of Bonaparte and Washington spread like wildfire through the Territory, back to Washington, DC, and across the Atlantic to the courts of Europe.

Murat's new relationship forced him to pay a little more attention to his personal appearance and his habit of chewing tobacco. When his future mother-in-law, Mary Willis, complained about the brown spots on the floor, he brought a shaggy dog along with him on visits and used the animal's coat for a spittoon. (NB: This same Mary Willis, granddaughter of George Washington's sister Betty, died in Pensacola in 1834 and is confirmed as buried in Pensacola's St John's historic Cemetery (Block 2 North, Section 19, Lot 23. Originally buried in a private cemetery, she and family members were re-interred at St. Johns in 1899. This close descendant of the illustrious Washington Family is one of Pensacola's most historic burials.)

Mary Willis Lewis, the granddaughter of George Washington's sister Betty, married George Barkley's business associate Byrd Charles Willis and moved to the Florida Territory with him and their nine children. They lived both in Tallahassee and Pensacola where they are closely affiliated with the Barkley family.
In 1834 she succumbed to yellow fever in Pensacola and was originally buried in a family cemetery. Her remains were re-interred in St. John's Cemetery, Pensacola in 1899, where her previously anonymous grave was affirmed by cemetery and historical records and a new memorial stone emplaced in 2005. Her grandson, Byrd Charles Willis II would later marry Lucy Rose Barkley, eldest daughter of George and Clara Barkley and forever link the Barkley family to that of George Washington.

Floridians were fascinated with the idea that if the Bonaparte forces on the continent managed to wangle a return to power, the Virginia-born-Florida-girl Kate could become queen, if not empress of a resurgent Bonaparte empire. She was, after all, marrying a member of the Bonaparte family and son of a Bonapartist king. There were few, if any, claimants to the mantle of the great Napoleon with higher claims on that legacy.

To the excitement of townspeople, Charles Louis Napoleon Achille Murat, nephew of Napoleon, son of a king, and himself the former crown prince of Naples, and Catherine Daingerfield Willis Grey were married on July 21, 1826, a few days after Tallahassee observed the 50th anniversary of American independence.

Despite the international attention focused on the event, the Tallahassee *Democrat* reported in subdued tone *"On Tuesday, the 21st of July, 1826, at Tallahassee, by Ed. Van Evans, justice of the peace, Achille Murat, Esq., late of Italy, eldest son of King Joachim, of Naples to Mrs. Catherine Daingerfield Gray, late of Fredericksburg, Va. and daughter of Byrd C. Willis."* It is reported in the French language volume *"Achille Murat en Belgique; un Citouyen Americain au Service de Notre Revolution"*, by Maurice-A Arnold (Brussels, 1938) that the illustrious hero of the American Revolution, the Marquis de Lafayette, who had been tendered lands in the new Florida Territory, and who was an intellectual and political patron of Murat, attended the wedding.

"Lipona", their plantation 15 miles from town on Moore Branch, near present- day Wacissa, became the social center for guests from Tallahassee and the surrounding plantations.

Though a crude approximation of a salon as known in Europe, it's social prominence rose to a level of sophistication which seems completely incongruous to the log cabin structure. Linens offered to guests bore the beautiful coat of arms from the lost kingdom, and gold spoons were marked with the crests of royalty; some from Napoleon himself and some from Kate's father-in-law, the late King Joachim.

Guests dined on tiny cakes and sweets in a rustic parlor that opened onto a verandah then strolled into large square garden, planted with orange trees and vines. Kate always appeared elegant and went about her daily life with the ladylike manners of her aristocratic upbringing in the high society of Virginia.

Murat remained a charming conversationalist but apparently vacillated between the sophisticate of royal pedigree and the coarse maven of the Florida frontier. He took great interest in the natural sciences and had every opportunity to attain success in many different fields but always seemed to blunder in his endeavors. No doubt this product of royalty, who spent his boyhood in the Elysee Palace was a cultural mismatch for rustic "Cracker" Florida frontier.

Some judged him more harshly, and blamed his eccentricities by noting that he was as fond of frontier homebrew as he was of the fine wines of his courtly upbringing.

Tales of Murat's unusual ways fueled talk for years and became legendary in the annals of frontier Florida. In a duel in 1826, the prince lost the tip of his finger over a difference in politics. Duelling, remember, was endemic in that era, and we have previously examined two dueling occasions involving Murat's presumed colleague and the protagonist of this book, George Barkley. Murat's connection to the Garnier family, Barkley's in-laws, is the reason why we devote this much time to the character of Murat which has been otherwise well-researched and much written about.

Achille Murat's eccentricities were many and legendary. This former royal colleague of George Barkley had some strange ways indeed, belying his royal upbringing! Ellen Call Long wrote in an article issued by the *Florida Historical Review* in 1867, that once when Achille Murat accidentally fell into a syrup vat and was pulled out a sticky mess, he lamented that Kate would force him to take a bath. Another time while Kate was away visiting neighbors, guests came to call. When Murat found no meat in the kitchen, he ordered his slaves to cut off all the ears and tails of his hogs so he could prepare a meal. The guests dined on his savory fare covered with strange sauces while his bloodied animals roamed the grounds. Whenever he experimented with plants and trees for their medicinal qualities and dyeing properties, Murat encouraged his wife to visit friends. One day she arrived back home to find her husband at work over a kettle in the yard with all her undergarments and dresses dyed a rosy pink. But the insatiable Murat remained restless, attempting one enterprise after another in his quest for wealth, railing all the while at the fates which had deprived him of the immense fortunes of his family. He also longed for the children the couple never had, and their barren marriage haunted Achille and Kate all of their lives.

Prince Murat, ever fascinated with the forms and processes of government, and well versed in the Napoleonic Codes which, alone in America, were in effect in Louisiana. Murat moved to New Orleans for a time where he was the law partner of Charles Garnier, brother of Pensacola's Clara Garnier

Barkley, the wife of George Barkley. This is strong evidence of the bonds between the Garniers and Murats. Napoleon's nephew was unquestionably a political bedfellow of the Garniers of both Pensacola and New Orleans, who like him, schemed to return the House of Bonaparte to power. Though lost to history, it is at least possible that Murat's move to Florida was abetted by the Garnier family who like Achille, were political exiles seeking a fresh start.

Linkage of the Families of George Barkley's Wife Clara Louise Garnier to the Families of the Murats and Bonapartes.

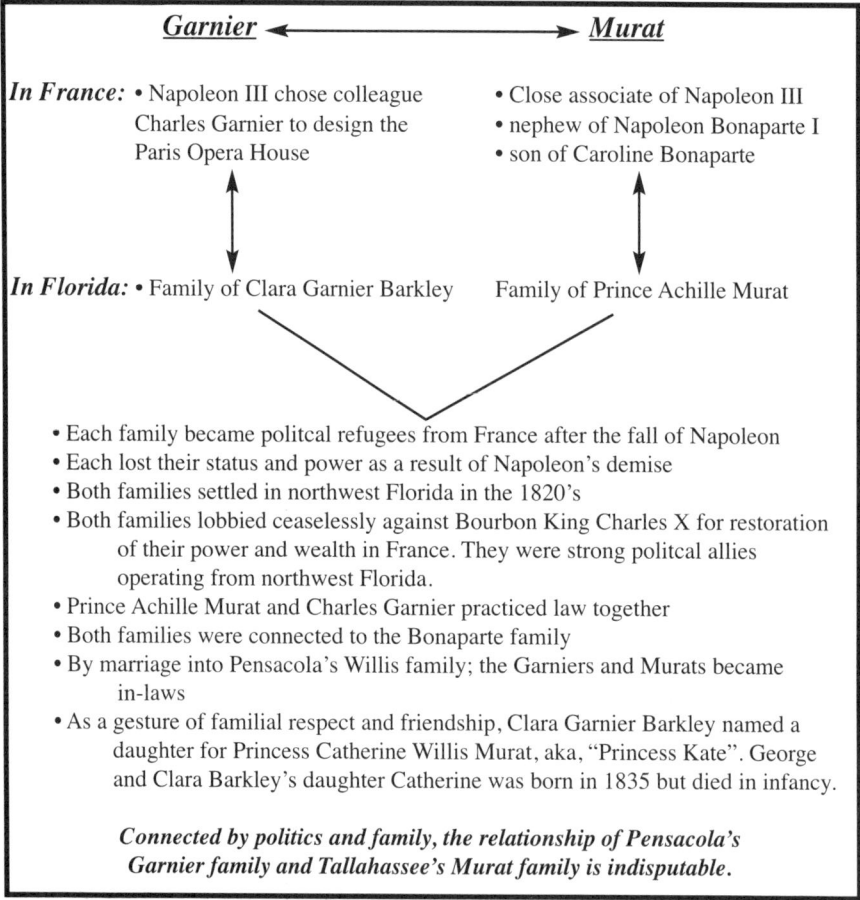

Garnier ⟵⟶ *Murat*

In France: • Napoleon III chose colleague Charles Garnier to design the Paris Opera House

• Close associate of Napoleon III
• nephew of Napoleon Bonaparte I
• son of Caroline Bonaparte

In Florida: • Family of Clara Garnier Barkley   Family of Prince Achille Murat

• Each family became politcal refugees from France after the fall of Napoleon
• Each lost their status and power as a result of Napoleon's demise
• Both families settled in northwest Florida in the 1820's
• Both families lobbied ceaselessly against Bourbon King Charles X for restoration of their power and wealth in France. They were strong politcal allies operating from northwest Florida.
• Prince Achille Murat and Charles Garnier practiced law together
• Both families were connected to the Bonaparte family
• By marriage into Pensacola's Willis family; the Garniers and Murats became in-laws
• As a gesture of familial respect and friendship, Clara Garnier Barkley named a daughter for Princess Catherine Willis Murat, aka, "Princess Kate". George and Clara Barkley's daughter Catherine was born in 1835 but died in infancy.

Connected by politics and family, the relationship of Pensacola's Garnier family and Tallahassee's Murat family is indisputable.

Such kindred spirits made Prince Murat and the Garnier's natural partners in political fervor, plotting and hiding out on the American frontier from the powers that swept over the continent on the falling tide of Napoleon. The leaders of those many and diverse European powers would have gladly executed either man had they not sought safety in America. These common threats and shared political aspirations bound Florida's Murat's and Garniers, George Barkley's inlaws, together, and in turn bound them to hopes that from the ashes of Napoleon's defeated empire a new opportunity would arise and restore their names, power, and fortunes.

The mercurial Achille Murat, exiled from power in Europe, had a penchant for playing both ends against the middle. While vociferously defending American-style democratic forms of government, he most assuredly would have enthusiastically taken up the mantle of imperial (eg, Bonapartist) power if it had come his way. When he made his dramatic and wholly unlawful return to Europe, he no doubt was watching the eclipse of the last French Bourbon monarchy as Charles X's power slipped away. Charles was the brother of both the now-executed King Louis XVI as well as the post-Napoleonic King Louis XXVIII, not to mention, an uncle to the young Louis XVII. Crowned in 1824, Charles presided over some of France's most politically convoluted years. When he dissolved his council of deputies in 1829, young Achille Murat smelled blood, returning secretively to the continent. No doubt in league with his cousin Louis Phillipe, Murat played a waiting game. His gamble appeared to payoff when Charles X abdicated to his grandson and the Chamber of Deputies refused to confirm him as Henri V, simultaneously declaring the French throne vacant, and elevating Achille Murat's cousin, Louis-Phillipe to power; later to become the self-styled Emperor Napoleon III. With a cousin on the throne, Murat, the unlikely political wild card... landowner of the Florida frontier and colleague of George and Clara Barkley... was sorely disappointed when cousin Louis Phillippe turned against him and the Murat claims summarily dismissed. He would later write to his friend and Tallahassee neighbor Colonel James Gadsden that "...unless we have war or some new incident in the affairs of Europe, wich (sic) I cannot foresee, the cause of liberty is lost. It has been infamously betrayed by those who have profited most by it. The names of Louis-Phillippe and his ministers will be handed down in history died (sic; he meant "dyed") with blacker infamy than almost any other."

The above descriptions may mean little in relation to Pensacola history until one recalls that Murat was linked in law practice with Clara Garnier Barkley's brother and was married to Catherine Willis; daughter of Pensacola's Byrd and Mary Willis. All orbited the Barkleys and their house by the bay.

It is tantalizing to peer into the dark crystal ball of undocumented history, teased by so many hints of the Garnier-Murat connection. They were political allies. There was family intermarriage through the well-placed Willis family, descendants of Washington. Both the Garniers and Murats were in Florida at the same time. They practiced law together and invested together. The question which remains unanswered by all research to date is this: Was the Garnier family which fled France affiliated with the royal Murats in Europe before each fled to America? Did the collapse of the Napoleonic Empire prompt John Garnier's flight to Pensacola in addition to the flight of Napoleon's nephew to Tallahassee? Did each family choose New Orleans by mere coincidence? Or, as the Empire tumbled about them, did Murat and Garnier plan to re-group on the Gulf coast, and plot, with others, a resurgence of some kind of neo-Bonapartist regime in Europe? How was it that a Murat-Garnier legal partnership sprang up?

The timing for speculating about a pre-existing relationship in Europe is exactly right. As far as we know John Garnier left France in the time frame 1816, give or take a year. Was this in some way related to Napoleon's defeat at Waterloo and second abdication in 1815? Garnier's immigration to the United States was followed in 1822 by Achille Murat and both ended up in northwest Florida.

Napoleon's death in exile occurred in 1821. John Garnier shows up in Pensacola in self-imposed exile from France in 1821. No mention of a Garnier role in the affairs of Napoleon I appears in any reference found to date, but like other parts of this fragmented tale, circumstance casts suggestions in that direction. If not high enough in the Napoleonic pecking order to warrant mention in the history books, it is still possible that John (Jean!) Garnier may have been a minor government functionary, perhaps somehow involved with the judicial system under Bonaparte as he was later in Pensacola under President Andrew Jackson. If so, he found himself on the wrong side of the law when the Bonaparte fortunes went into eclipse. We know that John Garnier had legal training, and at least one reference calls him "Judge Garnier." He served at Andrew Jackson's appointment in judicial positions in Pensacola.

Coincidence? Speculation? Or merely one more fact lost in the sandpile of history. Whatever it is, it offers another tantalizing historic possibility in close relation to George and Clara Garnier Barkley and their historic Pensacola home.

Did Prince Murat Spend Time at the Barkley House? With Clara Garnier Barkley's brother Charles Garnier in law practice in New Orleans with Napoleon's exiled nephew Prince Murat, and with the family of Murat's wife in residence on Pensacola's Bayou Chico, it is a near certainty that the Prince visited Pensacola and the Barkley House on the route from his plantation in Tallahassee to his law practice in New Orleans.

That the Prince of Naples and his wife Princess Kate frequented the Barkley House is one of the most tantalizing tales of the house. Like other notables who were most likely guests at the Barkley House, the case for the Murat-Barkley connection lacks proof, but is strongly suggested by circumstantial evidence. It is intriguing today to speculate that Pensacola's French-exile Garniers and the equally exiled nephew of Napoleon may even have dreamed of the restoration of the Bonaparte fortunes from the Barkley House! We shall add another few ounces to the weight of this evidence a few paragraphs below.

Murat and Garnier Connect Family Intermarriage. We know that in Tallahassee, on July 21, 1826, Prince Murat married Virginia-born Catherine Daingerfield Willis, great-grand niece of George Washington and young widow of the late Atchison Gray. In a twist of circumstance, the father of Catherine Willis was none other than George Barkley's business associate, Colonel Byrd Charles Willis, Jacksonian political appointee in Pensacola and the local brickyard owner whose brick may have been used in construction of the Barkley House.

In marrying Prince Murat, Catherine Willis became something of a celebrity. In a unique convergence of royalty and genealogy this same Catherine Willis, daughter of Pensacola's Colonel Byrd Charles Willis, became a "double princess", first of the lost Napoleonic Kingdom of Naples, and secondly, when she was summoned back to France by Emperor Napoleon III and created a princess of France's Second Empire. By the intermarriage of the Murat and Willis families, moreover, the Washington family of America and the fabled House of Bonaparte were united. This poignant story is told in Celia Myrover Robinson's classic *Jackson and the Enchanted City, Stories of Old Pensacola.* (Page 93)

"On one occasion while visiting an art gallery in London, in company with John Randolph and other distinguished personages, the party (which included Catherine Willis Murat) stopped before the pictures of Napoleon and Washington which hung side by side. Randolph, pointing to the picture, remarked, "Before us we have Napoleon and Washington, one the founder of a mighty empire, the other of a great republic;" then turning to the company said, "Behold in the Princess Murat the niece of both, a distinction which she alone can claim."

Catherine Daingerfield Willis, later elevated to the status of Princess of France by Emperor Napoleon III, was the daughter of Pensacola brick maker Colonel Byrd Charles Willis. She was fondly addressed as Princess Kate on both sides of the Atlantic. Though a princess of senior rank in the court of Napoleon III, she turned down a chateau and permanent position at court. Princess Catherine Willis Murat lived in Tallahassee and frequently visited her family in Pensacola, where she no doubt spent much time at the Barkley House.

In time, long after the fall of Napoleon I, the now-enthroned Emperor Napoleon III, out of friendship and gratitude for the Murat's support during his dark days, recalled Catherine Willis Murat to France from her Tallahassee home, and created her a Princess of France, where she was adoringly addressed as "Princess Kate." She was a special favorite of Emperor Napoleon III's wife, the Empress Eugenie. On one memorable occasion, at a glittering state dinner, in a gesture of exquisite courtesy the Empress Eugenie absented herself from the table, leaving Princess Kate the ranking nobility. Kate, daughter of a Pensacola brick maker, was then elevated to the throne of the Empress of the Second Empire, if only for the evening. After the event, Eugenie welcomed Kate in the royal apartments as a sister.

Empress Eugenie de Montijo, wife of Emperor Napoleon III, was a close friend of Barkley associate Princess Kate. The two spent much time together in the Tuileries, but Princess Kate declined the grant of a chateau and permanent appointment to the court of France in order to return to northwest Florida.

Emperor Napoleon III appointed Catherine Willis Murat, daughter of Pensacola brick maker Byrd Charles Willis, a princess of France. It is a virtual certainty that she spent substantial time at the Barkley House and it is believed that one of the Barkley daughters was named for her. Emperor Napoleon III also appointed a member of the Garnier family to design the famous Paris Opera House. Clara Louise Garnier of Bordeaux married George Barkley and was the "First Lady" of Pensacola's Barkley House. Both Garniers and Murats were closely connected to the emperor and empress.

Emperor Napoleon III offered this daughter of Pensacola brickmaker Byrd Charles Willis a lifetime stipend, permanent support in France, together with a chateau if she would remain on as a member of his court. She declined all of the Emperor's offers except the stipend and use of the royal livery of France in order to return to her beloved United States, land of her birth, and home of her family. Princess Kate lived out her days in Tallahassee, where her modest home "Belle Vue" is on display at the Florida Museum of Natural Science and History. "Belle Vue" had been built in 1825 for Samuel DuVal, nephew of the Governor, and his wife Ellen Willis, yet another daughter of Pensacola brick maker Byrd Charles Willis. Princess Kate thus assumed ownership of "Belle Vue", her Tallahassee home, from her sister.

For several years Prince and Princess Murat, who were associates and later in-laws of Pensacola's Barkley family, defied the ban on their return to the continent, sailed back to Europe and lived in the Hotel Belle Vue in Brussels (shown above). At that time Prince Murat, heir apparent to the Bonaparte empire, schemed for it's restoration. King Leopold of Belgium appointed Murat, now a Florida's landowner and married to Pensacola's Catherine Willis, as commander of his Belgian foreign legion. Soldiers of the disbanded armies of his uncle, Napoleon I, flocked to his banner. The legion was soon disbanded due to political pressure from the crowned heads of Europe, preventing these associates of George and Clara Barkley from mounting a serious resurgence of Bonaparte power.

Upon her return from the court of Napoleon III, Princess Catherine Willis Murat... "Princess Kate"... bought this simple plantation house outside Tallahassee. Princess Kate wistfully named her simple cracker home Belle Vue in memory of happy times living at the elegant Hotel Belle Vue in Brussels with her husband, Prince Murat. This simple structure, the home of a princess, still stands and is a part of the Tallahassee Museum of Natural Science and History. By this time her mother was buried in a private Pensacola cemetery, her father had returned to Virginia, but siblings remained in Pensacola.

Supported by a stipend from the Emperor Napoleon III, Pensacola daughter Princess Kate supported many charitable public causes and even helped save for posterity the famous home of her great uncle... Mount Vernon. Kate is buried in Tallahassee's St. John's Cemetery beside her Prince, Achille Murat... the enigmatic colleague of Pensacola's Garnier family. Kate's mother, wife of brick maker Byrd Charles Willis, lies in a simple grave in Pensacola's St. John's Cemetery. With political, business, and family connections, there is little doubt that "Princess Kate" would have spent substantial time at the Barkley House from nearby Tallahassee at some point in her extraordinary life...a chapter in the storied Barkley House's history not previously told, but surely supported by the evidence.

As was described in the foreword, this effort to illuminate early Pensacola lives hoped to portray them as a web of relationships. You have seen some examples of that already, as in the paragraph immediately above. Building on the Murat connection to the Garniers and to George Barkley, it enlightens the tale to develop yet another relationship that ties them all together.

Some pages before we showed how the families of George and Clara Garnier Barkley were aligned with Prince Achille Murat and his wife Princess Kate. Immediately above we saw how Achille Murat's wife, princess of France Catherine Willis Murat, "Princess Kate" was adored by

Emperor Napoleon III and the Empress Eugenie. We can develop the web of relationships of early Pensacolians further, demonstrating that Pensacola's Garniers were also linked directly to the House of Bonaparte, as well as through the Murats and Willises.

Just above we examined a relationship between Pensacola's Princess Kate and Napoleon III. Napoleon III had grandiose plans for his capital city, Paris, "The City of Light." When he sought a leading architect for his opus project, a new opera house for Paris, he chose none other than a member of the Garnier family. The elegant Paris Opera house today is still known as the Palais de Garnier, (see page 40) and it will be remembered that George Barkley married into that family.

A convoluted web of relationships. Politics. Duels. The breathtaking audacity of Napoleon's empire; in fact the breathtaking audacity of TWO Napoleonic empires!…the First and Second. Boiled owls in frontier Florida. Glittering royalty. A Pensacola brick maker from Virginia. A princess of France from Pensacola. The Washington family, first in the hearts of his countrymen. Exiled French aristocracy selling timber and coffee. The king of Naples. Andrew Jackson. Wine from a slipper in Tallahassee. Napoleonic tableware and linens used in a log cabin in "Cracker" Florida. *Our heads are spinning! Where is the common denominator?*

ALL OF THESE HAVE CONNECTIONS TO
PENSACOLA'S BELOVED BARKLEY HOUSE!

Why So Much About the Murats When They Were Not Pensacolians? One may well wonder why a book about the Barkleys and the history of Pensacola devotes so much time to the Murats and their in-laws, the Bonapartes. Napoleon's nephew Prince Achille Murat and his wife Catherine (Willis) Murat, niece of George Washington, are well known and well documented in Tallahassee, and much celebrated there in local lore, houses and land records, museum collections, and even the names of contemporary motels. In territorial times the Murats enjoyed a sort of rock-star status in Tallahassee, but their Pensacola connections are less well known. Notwithstanding, this illustrious couple and their connections to the houses of Bonaparte and Washington respectively is conclusively linked to Pensacola.

If they are so famous, one wonders why that tale is less well known as a part of Pensacola history, and why the Murat connections to Pensacola are told here for the first time?

THE PRINCE, THE PRINCESS, AND PENSACOLA

Prince and Princess Murat, well known in Tallahassee and St. Augustine, also had strong but little known connections to Pensacola.

Princess Murat's family lived on Bayou Chico in Pensacola. Her father was President Andrew Jackson's representative at the Pensacola Navy Yard. The princess returned to France at the invitation of Napoleon III accompanied by her Pensacola nephew. Her sister married the commandant of the Pensacola Navy Yard. Her mother, who was the granddaughter of George Washington's sister Betty, is buried in Pensacola's St. John's Cemetery.

Prince Murat, son of Caroline Bonaparte, maintained a strong relationship with the family of Clara Garnier Barkley, and practiced law with Clara's brother. With Napoleon in exile, the Pensacola Garniers and Prince Murat, resident of Tallahassee, found common cause in the dream of a resurgence of Bonaparte power. He had close personal ties to Pensacola attorney Richard Keith Call and to James Gadsden; each prominent in Pensacola. His father-in-law was a Pensacola brick maker.

The Murats had no children, but many collateral descendants of this family of Bonaparte ancestry still populate the port city.

In part their conspicuous absence from traditional Pensacola history is because their relationship to Pensacola was one which left no physical evidence or monuments to their international status. In Pensacola, the Murat tale is one of intangible human relationships, not of brick-and-mortar tangibles such as ownership of property or gravesites as found in Tallahassee. The only physical evidence of a Pensacola Murat connection is a newly placed grave marker at Pensacola's St. John's Cemetery memorializing the burial of Princess Murat's mother, Mary W. Willis. It is emplaced at the head of her original slab which is so weathered as to be illegible. Princess Murat's mother was reinterred at St. Johns in 1899 from an earlier burial site in a family cemetery, and her new stone indeed evidences that Princess Murat was not only an occasional figure in early Pensacola history, but that the port city was her family's home.

Too, the Pensacola connections of the Murats were transitory; mere grains of sand in the hourglass of history. But in the 1830's and 40's one may safely conclude that these royals... Napoleon's nephew the prince of Naples and his wife, a princess of France, and their respective family legacies indeed were woven into events in Pensacola, bringing with them their historic connections of international significance. Indeed had fate taken a different turn and pro-Bonapartist sympathizers regained control on the continent, the deposed Prince Murat, law partner of Clara Garnier Barkley's brother, and Murat's wife Kate, daughter of a Pensacola brick maker, were in line of succession to assume the mantles of emperor and empress in the event of a revival of Bonaparte power. With hindsight of course we known that such grandiose dreams were not to be, but the potential of a Bonaparte renaissance and the chance to vindicate his father's death haunted Prince Murat for many years. These altruistic goals would have been accompanied of course by great wealth and power had Prince Murat contrived to reestablish Napoleon's lost empire. It was always a far-fetched possibility, but this unlikely couple, with connections to Pensacola, conceivably might have followed in the imperial footsteps of his uncle Napoleon; a far cry from rustic "cracker" Florida where these dreams incubated.

If there was one single locus for the Murat connections to Pensacola, one may safely deduce that it was the Barkley House. At Pensacola's Barkley House, the Murats had political, professional, and familial ties to both the Garniers (Barkley in-laws) and to the Willises; the same Willises who intermarried with both the Barkley and Murat lines.

The foregoing pages detailing Murat connections shine a light on a historic drama of early Pensacola history which has heretofore been seen through a glass darkly, if at all. Surely Pensacola's already rich history takes on even more luster when enfolded with the colossal, inestimably important histories of the houses of Bonaparte and of Washington, and that is the basis for the foregoing extensive detail.

Barclay (Barkley) and Murat; Cohorts in Florida; Enemies in Europe. Barclay Versus Murat; a Supreme Irony of Fate.

Substantial new research has shown in this book the heretofore untold story of Prince Achille Murat and the families of George W. Barkley of Pensacola's Barkley House, and how they were related in business and politics, and even shared common in-laws. The exiled prince, as a nephew of Napoleon was often considered first-among-equals as a contender for the Bonaparte throne. As nephew of Napoleon and a favored family member, at one time Achille Murat, colleague of many of the early settlers of northwest Florida discussed in this book, stood squarely in the potential line of succession to the Napoleonic Empire, either directly or, more provocatively, as a successor to resurgent Bonapartist political power while Uncle Napoleon himself languished in exile. Betrayal was nothing new to the Murat's, for such betrayal had led to the execution of his father by firing squad in Pizzo, Italy.

Had Achille Murat ever pulled off his unlikely dream of the mantle of empire, his American bride, Catherine Willis Murat whose father served as Andrew Jackson's agent at the Pensacola Navy Yard, later a princess of France in her own right, would in that event have achieved a status totally unprecedented in history before or since; an American born empress.

In that fanciful dream of Achille Murat, one of the land masses which he and Princess Murat might have ruled, but for the defeat of Napoleon's *Grande Armee* was the vast expanse of Russia and here the fates played out one of history's great ironies.

Northwest Florida's Prince Achille Murat was, as noted earlier, the son of Napoloeon's greatest cavalry commander, Marshal, later king of Naples, Joachim Murat. As Napoleon's massive army pressed ever deeper into Russia in 1812, it was increasingly subject to attack of its logistical lines to the rear by Cossack raids. Allowing Napoleon to overextend his line of communication, rather than meet him head on in decisive strategic battle, was in early 1812 an effective strategy for the Russians under their Minister of War, Prince Mikhail Barclay de Tolly, a Scotsman whose family had settled in the region of Livonia in the 17th Century. Barclay de Tolly, curiously, was a member of the same Clan Barclay as Pensacola's George W. Barkley, and was in fact a collateral ancestor.

As the *Grande Armee* of Napoleon neared Moscow however, Barclay de Tolly was relieved of overall command, and the Russian main force, now under Field Marshal Kutusov, prepared the carefully selected ground at Borodino for decisive engagement. Prince Mikhail Barclay de Tolly, collateral ancestor of George Barclay (*cum* Barkley) of Pensacola; of the Clan Barclay remained at Borodino to command the Russian right wing.

On September 7, 1812 more than a quarter of a million men collided in massive engagement at Borodino. For Napoleon, Marshal Joachim Murat, as was his style, led from the front, white ostrich plumes billowing. His thundering cavalry charge of more than 15,000 men, characteristically impetuous, overwhelmed the *fleche* defenses of Barclay de Tolly, setting the stage for the Russian's strategic retreat to Moscow. The principal passages of Tchaikowsky's famous *1812 Overture* celebrate Murat's thundering charge that fated day, memorializing in one of the world's most recognized musical works, the audacious leadership of Marshal Murat.

But misery rather than glory awaited as Napoloeon's forces moved on Moscow. There the Russian scorched earth policy laid torch to their own capital city, but enticed a frustrated Napoleon to remain until the advent of the fierce winter which doomed the *Grande Armee* and killed most of it during the inglorious frozen retreat. As Napoleon gloomily abandoned his dreams of conquest amidst the bitter Russian winter, he turned once again to Marshal Murat to shepherd the remains of his once invincible army to a semblance of safety.

Field Marshal Prince Mikhail Barclay de Tolly, a kinsman of George W. Barkley, commanded Russian forces at the battle of Borodino, opposing Marshal Joachim Murat, commander of Napoleon's cavalry forces and father of Barkley cohort Prince Achille Murat. In an irony of history, Barclay de Tolly played a role in thwarting Prince Achille Murat's dreams of succession to the Bonaparte throne.

But herein lies the story as it relates to Pensacola and to this book.

In the act of the large scale combat at Borodino lay an irony of historic proportion, and one with incongruous implications for two historic figures of early Pensacola.

Prince Mikhail Barclay de Tolly, fellow member of George Barkley's Clan Barclay and a cousin, had met on the field of battle none other than the father in law of Pensacola's Princess Catherine Murat. Though de Tolly's battlefield withdrawal drew criticism in some quarters, the strategic retreat from Borodino to Moscow set the stage for the final defeat of Napoleon in Russia.

Had Napoleon succeeded in Russia and later conquests, and had Prince Achille Murat eventually followed his uncle Napoleon to power as many believed likely, the empire of Napoleon would have lain at his feet, and who knows if there would have been the ill-considered Battle of Waterloo to terminate it?

Instead of glory though, there lay in Prince Murat's future in just a few short years the execution of his father, a brooding self-imposed exile to the United States, and boiled owls in a log cabin on the Florida frontier.

And Achille Murat would never know that his Pensacola colleague George Barkley descended from the line of Barclays who defeated his father in Russia, blunted Napoleon's dreams of grandeur, and thwarted his own potential accession to the lofty crown of the Bonaparte empire. Irony indeed!

More Evidence of a Murat-Barkley Connection.   Further evidence of the extent of the Murat's affiliation with Pensacola is suggested in *Twentieth Century Biographical Dictionary of Notable Americans*, Volume III, Page 110. There one finds discussion of a nephew of Catherine Willis Murat, Trevanion Barlow Dallas. Trevanion was the son of Catherine's sister Mary and her husband, Alexander Dallas, former commandant of the Pensacola Navy Yard. With his parents and grandparents as residents of Pensacola, Trevanion was clearly a Pensacolian both during his youth and later under the command of General Chase, Pensacola's famed fort builder. Trevanion's mother, Mary Byrd Willis had moved to Pensacola in the 1820's with her family; father Colonel Byrd Charles Willis and mother Mary Lewis Willis, when they left Virginia following a financial collapse. In Pensacola she met and married Commodore Alexander J. Dallas; commandant of the Pensacola Navy Yard. From a manuscript written by Mary's father we get this beguiling human-level insight: *"At a "Bouquet Ball" at this place, Pensacola, Commodore A. J. Dallas was made King, he presented the bouquet to her, hence she was queen at a party given by the Commodore of the Navy Yard, May, 1833."* From this beginning, authoritatively observed and documented by her father, arose the marriage of Mary Byrd Willis to Commodore Dallas. This then places both Princess Murat's sister Mary Byrd (Willis) Dallas and her siblings in Pensacola along with her mother and father during the heyday of the Barkley House, which as we have noted above was most likely built, at least partially, of bricks from the yard owned by the Princess's father Colonel Byrd Charles Willis.

Barkley House Guest "Princess Kate" of French Nobility, Selected Her Pensacola Nephew to Accompany Her on Her Final Return to the Tuileries and France's Second Empire.

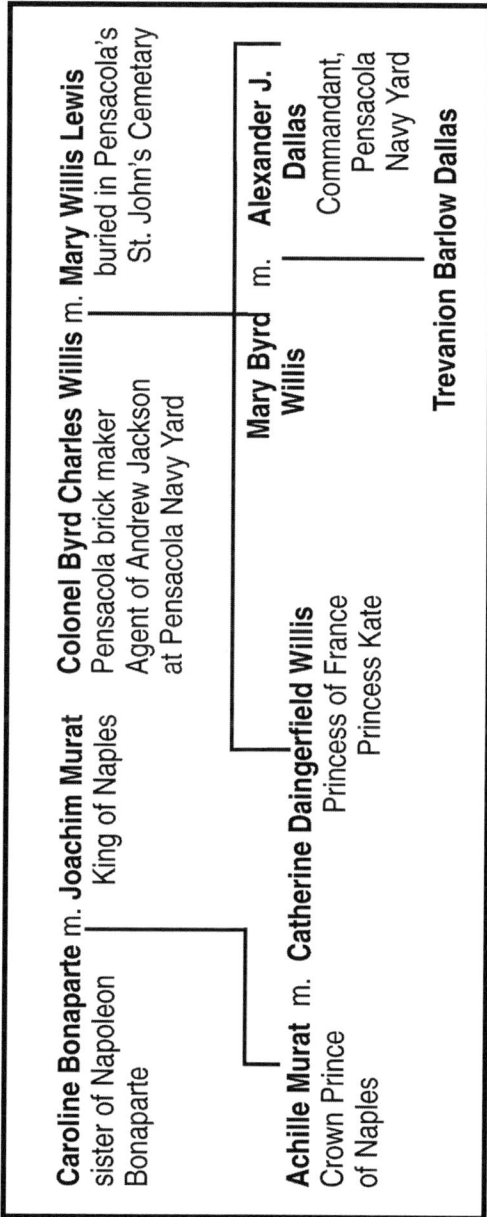

Caroline Bonaparte m. **Joachim Murat**
sister of Napoleon Bonaparte — King of Naples

Colonel Byrd Charles Willis m. **Mary Willis Lewis**
Pensacola brick maker, Agent of Andrew Jackson at Pensacola Navy Yard — buried in Pensacola's St. John's Cemetary

Achille Murat m. **Catherine Daingerfield Willis**
Crown Prince of Naples — Princess of France, Princess Kate

Mary Byrd Willis m. **Alexander J. Dallas**
Commandant, Pensacola Navy Yard

Trevanion Barlow Dallas

In old age "Princess Kate" selected her Pensacola nephew Trevanian Dallas to accompany her on her final visit to France and to her patron, Emperor Napoleon III. Throughout her life, "Princess Kate" frequented the Barkley House as both friend and in-law of the Barkley family.

Trevanion Dallas was the son of Princess Kate's (Catherine Willis Murat) sister Mary and her husband Commodore Alexander J. Dallas. The suggestion of strong family bonds between Princess Murat and her nephew, Pensacola's Trevanion Dallas, is revealing. Though Trevanion Dallas was 43 years younger than his aunt, the Princess Murat, he visited France with the Princess as her guest in 1865. In her mid-sixties at the time of this trip, the princess no doubt felt she needed an escort for the arduous journey from Florida to France and return. This trip occurred some 20 years after Prince Murat's death in 1845, and was the second time Princess Kate, daughter of a Pensacola brick maker, returned to France at the invitation of Emperor Napoleon III. If Princess Kate Murat were not in close contact with her Pensacola nephew, Trevanion, how did a royal trip of this magnitude come about? Evidence once again supports a view that the Murat family indeed had Pensacola ties. To sum up the evidence that the royal Murat family frequented the Barkley House, we have noted:

1. First, the intense and pervasive political and business connections of the Murats with Clara Garnier Barkley's exiled French family, the Garniers. It would have been normal, even expected, for Prince Murat to visit his partners family on the arduous trips between Tallahassee and New Orleans.

2. Second we have shown that Princess Kate, Catherine Daingerfield Willis Murat, was born Catherine Daingerfield Willis, daughter of George Barkley's business associate in Pensacola, Col. Byrd Charles Willis, and

3. Third, we have a record of Princess Murat's affinity for her Pensacola nephew, Trevanion Dallas and his parents (her sister and brother in law). A letter dated March 16, 1849, now in the DAR Museum in Washington written by Princess Murat to her brother contains the line *"...I have had the pleasure of having Mary Byrd Dallas and the children with me this winter. They are now in Pensacola...."* Mary Byrd Dallas was one of Byrd Charles Willis's daughters, who married Pensacola Navy Yard Commandant A.J. Dallas. The reference to "the children" would have included Trevanion who accompanied Princess Murat to France.

Well into her 60's, Catherine Willis Murat... "Princess Kate"... returned to Paris at the invitation of Napoleon III. Her escort for the voyage was her Pensacola nephew, Trevanion Barlow Dallas. Her deceased mother, Mary Willis, was at that time buried in a private family cemetery in the Cantonment area, but re-interred in 1899 in St. John's Cemetery where a new memorial marker was erected in 2005. Several of her brothers, sisters, nieces and nephews lived in Pensacola, and after her husband Prince Murat's death, "Princess Kate' spent more and more time in the port city. This is absolutely confirmed by correspondence in her own hand to her brother in 1849, complaining of expenses incurred in Pensacola. The previous winter in the same letter she describes corresponding with her mother-in-law, Queen (of Naples) Caroline Bonaparte Murat.

Shortly before this photograph of "Pensacola's princess" was made in Paris in the last year of her life, she was active in the Mount Vernon Ladies Association, and played an important role in saving the historic home of her great uncle, George Washington. In later years, Kate contributed generously to Confederate causes and fired the cannon at the Florida Statehouse signaling Florida's secession from the Union. "Princess Kate" died childless and is buried in Tallahassee's St. John's Cemetery beside her Prince, Achille Murat, of the Bonaparte family, while her mother, Mary Willis, is buried in Pensacola's St. Johns.

Though a Princess of France, this later-life photograph of Princess Kate accurately depicts her preference for simplicity over the glitter and pretension of courtly life. When her patron, Napoleon III offered her a chateau and a permanent position in his court, she declined in order to return to northwest Florida and the blessings of American democracy.

Murat-Garnier-Barkley Connections and Conjecture. Whether the volatile Prince Murat spent time at the Barkley House is conjectural but we believe it can be proven circumstantially if we assign correct meaning to a set of seemingly unrelated facts. The mercurial Murat had large land holdings at Tallahassee (his "Lipona" plantation) in addition to his law practice in New Orleans, and would have passed through Pensacola en route between the two. It is more than likely that such trips would have been made in the company of his partner in law and politics; Charles Garnier, brother of Clara Garnier Barkley. It is fascinating to imagine the nephew of Napoleon and son of King Joachim Murat gazing out upon Pensacola Bay from the welcoming verandas of the Barkley House, talking French politics with the sophisticated Garniers. Alas, we are left to wonder if this actually happened, but surely the ingredients for it were in place, and Prince Murat would have been quite at home in the Barkley House's milieu of aristocracy and frontier plainness.

Circumstantial evidence that Napoleon's nephew, Crown Prince of Naples Charles Louis Napoleon Achille Murat and his wife, French Princess Catherine Daingerfield Willis Murat, visited the Barkley house is both powerful and persuasive. Can we prove it 100%? No. But measured in probabilities, we believe that it is more probable than not that these royals spent time at the Barkley House participating in discussion with the Garniers about the changing face of Europe and prospects for a resurgent Bonaparte empire. We know that these dreams came to fruition with Emperor Napoleon III, though the Murat claims continued to be rejected. These connections to the empire of Napoleon Bonaparte and to later generations of French royalty provide a historic and heretofore neglected prism through which to view Pensacola's Barkley House. As host to descendants of both Napoleon and George Washington, we see George Barkley as more than a prominent Pensacola merchant. George Barkley's associates in fact comprised a network of power that spanned the Atlantic as well as territorial Florida and the United States.

How the Family of Princess Catherine Willis Murat Intermarried With Pensacola's Barkley Family. As we know the social uppercrust of Pensacola in the 1830's and 40's was small indeed. There can be no doubt that in that small community, George Washington's grand-nephew Colonel Byrd Charles Willis and Pensacola's George Barkley, both well-placed in Pensacola society, were social colleagues as well as business associates. We know that a business relationship between Willis and Barkley existed, with Barkley's schooner, the ALEXANDER OF PENSACOLA and sloop, YANKEE transporting bricks from Willis's Scenic Heights brickyard to both Mobile and New Orleans. It is said, only partly tongue-in-cheek, that New Orleans was built of Pensacola brick and George Barkley shipped some of it.

The Barkley Family Has Links to the Family of George Washington Through the Marriage of Their Daughter, Lucy Rose Barkley.

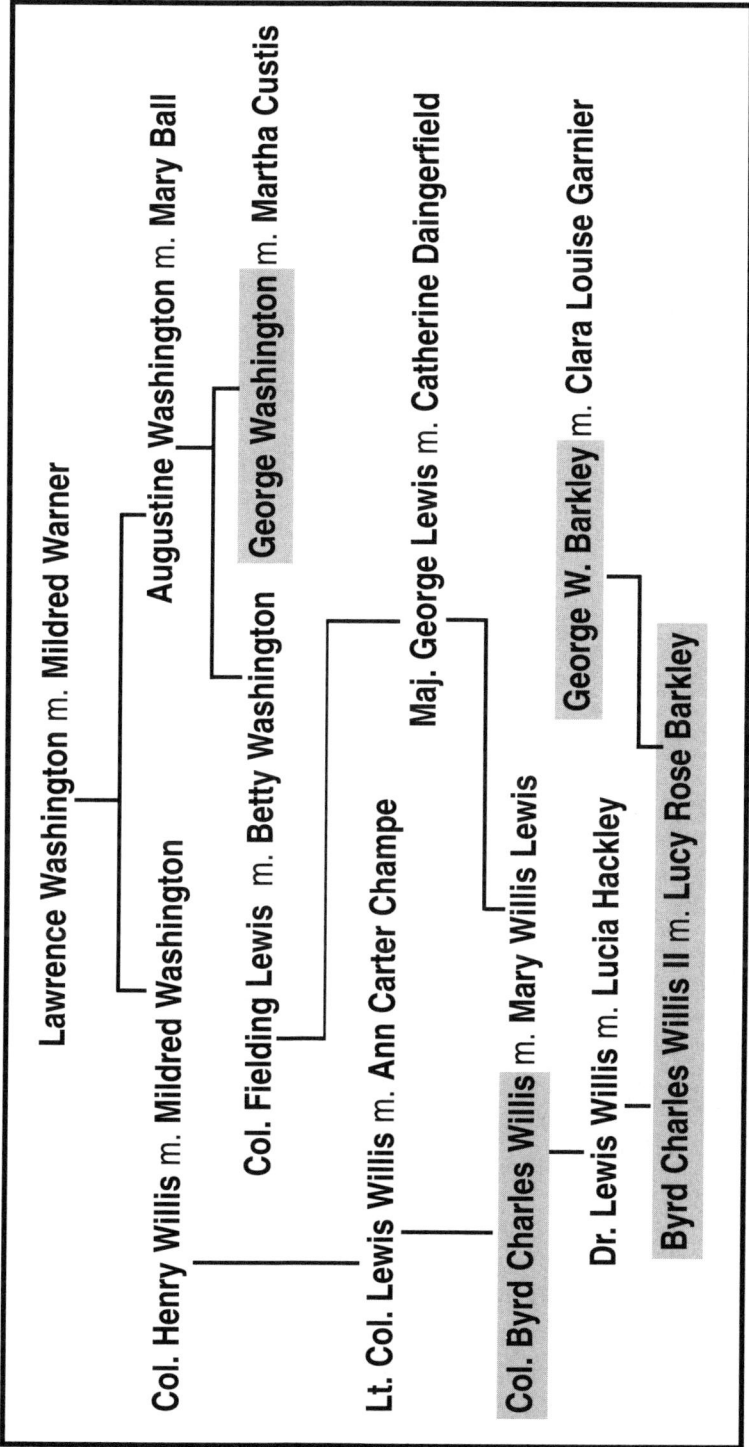

Lawrence Washington m. Mildred Warner

Augustine Washington m. Mary Ball

George Washington m. Martha Custis

Col. Henry Willis m. Mildred Washington

Col. Fielding Lewis m. Betty Washington

Maj. George Lewis m. Catherine Daingerfield

Lt. Col. Lewis Willis m. Ann Carter Champe

George W. Barkley m. Clara Louise Garnier

Col. Byrd Charles Willis m. Mary Willis Lewis

Dr. Lewis Willis m. Lucia Hackley

Byrd Charles Willis II m. **Lucy Rose Barkley**

In-law and business partner of George Barkley, Colonel Byrd Charles Willis and his wife Mary both brought the bloodlines of the Washington family to Pensacola. Willis served as Andrew Jackson's agent at the Pensacola Navy Yard during the late 1820's and 30's. He also was a prominent brick maker and colonel of the Florida militia.

In the museum of the Pensacola Historical Society one finds confirmation of the "B.C. Willis Brickyard" in the exhibit related to construction of Pensacola's fortifications; Barrancas, Pickens, and McRee.

A larger-than-life historic figure, Colonel Byrd Charles Willis had been born to aristocracy and wealth in 1781 at the family plantation, "Willis Hill" in Fredericksburg, VA. In this case 'larger than life" is both a literal as well as figurative description...he weighed some 350 pounds! When Colonel Willis married Mary W. Lewis in 1800, he married well. His bride's grandmother was none other than George Washington's sister, Betty. Since Washington left no offspring, this relationship was as close as you could get to the esteemed Washington, first president of the United States.

In a double relationship to the illustrious Washington family, Willis's own grandmother was Mildred Washington, wife of George Washington's father, Augustine. No one could claim more Washington blood than Colonel Byrd Charles Willis, Pensacola businessman, colleague of George Barkley, political appointee of President Andrew Jackson, and father of a princess of France! And he was a business associate of George Barkley.

Grandmother of Pensacola's Mary Willis... Betty Washington, sister of George Washington.

Colonel Byrd Charles Willis, once a wealthy Virginia blueblood, moved to the Florida Territory after losing his fortune. He was a close associate of Florida's first acting governor, Andrew Jackson, who may have induced the move and who appointed Willis as his agent at the Pensacola Navy Yard. Willis also owned a brick factory in northeast Pensacola near Mackey Bay and his in-law and close friend George Barkley shipped Willis's brick to market.

Willis is pictured here with his youngest son, Achille Murat Willis, named, at the behest of his daughter Princess Kate, for his son-in-law, the Crown Prince of Naples. The naming of this child was regarded as a way of preserving the Murat name since Achille and Catherine died childless.

This portrait of Colonel Byrd Charles Willis, in-law and friend of the Barkleys, is by artist Emmanuel Leutze, who painted the famous "Washington Crossing the Delaware". Speculation holds that Byrd Charles and his son "Little Mu", named for Achille Murat, sat for this portrait while visiting the estate of Napoleon's exiled brother Joseph Bonaparte in New Jersey, on the banks of the Delaware. Pensacola's Byrd Charles Willis and his family, while living in Pensacola, were guests at "Point Breeze", Joseph Bonaparte's estate at Bordentown, NJ. Joseph Bonaparte was the ex King of Spain when Willis visited him and sat for this portrait.

After business reversals in Virginia, Willis, as he says in an autobiography, *"sold off, paid off, and came off to this place, Florida."* What an adjustment that would have been, for he was of such aristocratic background that he was a politically connected Virginia blue-blood who drove his own coach-and-four, attired his staff in livery, plowed his field with thoroughbreds, and summered at the fashionable Fauquier White Sulphur Springs. To Colonel Willis is ascribed the reputation as the best known man in Virginia outside the small circle of government officials. His hospitality was legendary and he was not well liked by the tavern owners of Fredericksburg who complained that he competed with them for hospitality among friend and stranger alike.

Upon moving to the Florida Territory, Byrd Charles Willis settled first in Tallahassee, the capital, where he received his title of Colonel from appointment in the territorial militia. Shortly thereafter, Colonel Willis declined President Andrew Jackson's offer of a federal judgeship, but accepted Jackson's appointment at the Pensacola Navy Yard as his personal "agent", relocated to Pensacola with his family, and settled on Bayou Chico, which was at that time known as West Lagoon.

No positions comparable to "Navy agent" exist today...apparently a hybrid of political commissar, personal representative of the Commander in Chief, and comptroller responsible for the expenditure of federal funds; co-equal to rather than subordinate to the base commander.

No doubt this plum job was a 19th century political payoff, as Willis was a close friend of "Old Hickory" and instrumental in Jackson's election as seventh President of the United States.

One son of Byrd and Mary Willis, Doctor Lewis Willis, drowned in Grande Lagoon in 1835 and is buried in St. Johns cemetery, having been re-interred there with other family members in 1899. It is said that he drowned while trying to cross Grand Lagoon on horseback trying to reach a patient. Another Pensacola son, was George Willis, yet another colleague of George and Clara Barkley. A West Point graduate, George owned the escaped slaves abetted by Captain Jonathan Walker, a sea captain and abolitionist. History notes that George Willis pursued his slaves, aboard a US revenue cutter, on their ill fated voyage to Cuba captured the lot of them, and prosecuted Walker as a slave stealer. In the Pensacola courtroom where Jonathan Walker was tried and convicted in 1844, Walker's hand was branded with the initials "SS" (for slave stealer), later immortalized in Whittier's poem *"The Branded Hand."* George Barkley's son-in-law Sheriff Eben Dorr, did the branding. While slavery was legal during George Barkley's and his Willis colleagues entire lives, this barbaric event of the branding of a human being added fuel to the slavery controversy which would not be settled for decades to come.

Robert "King" Carter   William Byrd II

Pensacola brick maker and Andrew Jackson's agent at Pensacola Navy Yard, Byrd Charles Willis, a colonel of the Florida territorial militia, was a transplant-ed Virginia aristocrat who lived on Bayou Chico. The family tree of this Pensacolian of the 1830's included these two blue-blooded Virginians; his name-sake William Byrd II of "Westover" and Robert "King" Carter of "Corotoman"; both great grandparents of Willis. Scholars generally agree that "King" Carter was, with a plantation of over 300,000 acres, the wealthiest man in America.

"King" Carter's great grandson Colonel Willis however lost his Virginia fortune and made his way to Pensacola to start anew, bringing with him the sophistica-tion of his Virginia ancestry, and nine children whose descendants populate Pensacola today. When his wife Mary died of yellow fever in Pensacola in 1834 the Pensacola "Gazette" eulogized her lavishly. Re-interred in 1899 to St. John's Cemetery in 2005, Mayor John Fogg of Pensacola presided over the dedication of a new memorial to Mary Willis in 2005. She too, was a Virginia aristocrat, and a member of the Washington family.

Byrd Willis was a business and social colleague of George Barkley, builder of Pensacola's Barkley House. His namesake grandson, Byrd C. Willis II, married one of the Barkley daughters, Lucy Rose, in 1854 linking the Barkley family to these historic blue-blooded Virginians.

One of Byrd Charles Willis's sons and a brother to Princess Kate was George Willis, who owned the slaves who escaped with the help of Jonathan Walker. He followed the escaped slaves and apprehended them off the coast of Cuba. Willis had Walker arrested, and in a Pensacola courtroom, Walker's hand was branded "SS" (for slave stealer) giving rise to Whittier's poem, "The Branded Hand".

The Willis Brickyard. Colonel Byrd Charles Willis established his brickyard in the northeast environs of Pensacola, at Gulf Point facing Mackey Bay. The brickyard there had a long history dating back to the 1770's or earlier, and a brick kiln at Gulf Point is recorded on a British map dated 1780.

Willis joined forces in his brick making venture with Mr. Henry Slayback, late of Prussia, to manufacture brick for the construction of Pensacola's fortifications. In all likelihood the merger reflected Willises money and Slayback's knowledge, for nothing in Willises background suggest a knowledge of the industry. Perhaps the two sought to use Willis's influence and close relationship with President Andrew Jackson for an inside track to Federal contracts, for they were close and President Andrew Jackson owed Willis political favors stemming from his role in the Jackson candidacy and election. It was a cozy situation, fraught with conflict of interest. Willis's slaves made the brick, then Willis awarded himself the Navy contracts. After which Willis rented his slaves to the Navy Yard for construction. It is reliably said that Fort McRee at the mouth of Pensacola harbor, now lost to hurricane tides, was at least partly built of Willis brick. Some of those Willis-stamped brick are in possession of the Pensacola Historical Society.

It is this Byrd Charles Willis the brick maker with whom George W. Barkley had business and social relationships and a common interest in Christ Church. We may be 100% certain that Colonel Byrd Charles Willis and his wife Mary, the parents of Catherine Willis Murat "Princess Kate", of George Willis of "slave stealer" notoriety, of Dr. Lewis Willis who drowned in Grand Lagoon, and of Ellen Willis, in-law of Florida governor William DuVal doubtless frequented the Barkley House. These prominent Pensacolians, of Virginia birth, are not well known in Pensacola history, but were significant players in the social structure of the port city until Mary Willis's death on October 7, 1834, at which time the Pensacola *Gazette* wrote:

"We have lost a friend and the city has lost one of its brightest ornaments; a lady the centre of social attraction, one whose place will not soon be filled."

It is likely that she was felled by yellow fever or malaria, as the *Gazette's* writer goes on to extol the need for combatting these dread diseases.

Virginia aristocrat Mary Lewis Willis, granddaughter of George Washington's sister Betty, mother of Princess Murat, is buried in Pensacola in St. Johns Historic Cemetery, (Block 2 North, Section 19, Lot 23) where her remains were reinterred in 1899 from a private family cemetery. Though her very old tombstone is weathered away so as to be illegible, St. Johns Cemetery records confirm this as her burial site and a new marker has been emplaced by the Pensacola Chapter of the Sons of the American Revolution. Several of her children, including Dr. Lewis Willis who drowned in Grand Lagoon are interred beside her.

General Dabney Herndon Maury, who also started out life as a Virginian, recalls George Barkley's business associate Byrd Willis this way in his 1894 book *"Recollections of a Virginian in the Mexican, Indian, and Civil Wars".*

"Colonel Byrd Willis was one of the famous characters of his day. Connected with the most influential families of the State, he was the noted wit and *raconteur* of that old town. (Referring to Fredericksburg, Virginia.) Weighing over three hundred pounds, he might have played Falstaff without the padding, and in his geniality and kindness equalled Shakespeare's masterpiece. The charming Princess Achille Murat was his daughter. She was an ornament of the court of the third Emperor,..."

Clearly the Pensacola brick maker had led a life of privilege and status in Virginia before the collapse of his (sizeable) fortune and his relocation to the Florida Territory. As the granddaughter of George Washington's sister, his wife too bore the blue blood of the Old Dominion, bringing a unique level of sophistication and culture to the burgeoning port city of Pensacola in the 1820's and 30's.

Relatives of the Washington family. Relatives of the Bonapartes. A princess. Governors. Mayors. Distinguished authors. Legislators. Commodores. Such was the nature of the refined society which adorned the Barkley House in its heyday.

After his wife Mary's death, a despondent Colonel Byrd Charles Willis left Pensacola to return to familiar Virginia where he died October 1, 1846. There the gregarious, overweight Pensacola brick maker, colleague of George and Clara Barkley, descendant of the Washington family and father of French nobility is buried in the Willis family graveyard on the grounds of "Willis Hill", his boyhood home overlooking Fredericksburg. Evidence of the close relationship of the Willises with the Washington family is clear: Betty Washington's own son is buried beside Byrd Charles Willis in the private Willis graveyard.

"Willis Hill" was later renamed Marye's Heights. Less than 20 years after Byrd Charles Willis's burial there, shot and shell raked the site of his burial in one of the bloodiest battles of the Civil War during the siege of Fredericksburg, his tombstone itself scarred by the combat.

From the close Pensacola relationship of Barkley and Willis and their families and children, there arose a romantic interest. The talented and refined Barkley daughter Lucy Rose, was later to marry the grandson of Colonel Byrd Charles Willis, Byrd Charles Willis II. All the while, Colonel Willis' daughter Catherine (Kate), of the Court of Emperor Napoleon II, had been elevated as to the role of the Princess Murat, wife of Achille Murat, who practiced law with Clara Garnier Barkley's brother, Charles. (Refer to the paragraphs above concerning Prince Achille Murat.) All in all, it was a tangled web of aristocracy, intermarriage, politics on both sides of the Atlantic, and a succession of businesses, played out in part in Pensacola's historic treasure, the Barkley House!

Lucy Rose Barkley Willis,
wife of Byrd Charles Willis II.

Byrd Charles Willis II, grandson of the
Byrd Charles Willis who was a
business associate of George Barkley.

Other Historic Legacies of the Barkley House. There being no records and no living witnesses, we must use the few scant facts we have and extrapolate those with a bit of reasoning to deduce the other historic persons who likely played out some part of Pensacola's history at the Barkley House. We know, for example that General William C. Chase was constructing Pensacola's harbor fortifications at the same time the Barkley's were prominent leaders of Pensacola, and we know that Barkley transported brick for Chase's historic forts which provided the defenses for the port city. It would be more than reasonable to suggest that General Chase and George Barkley, each a leader in early Pensacola, enjoyed a social relationship as well as a business one.

Surely we could infer that Mayor Charles Evans, who on July 31, 1824 appointed Barkley as city treasurer and tax collector, would have enjoyed the hospitality of the Barkleys at their home on the bay.

For a time, the record shows that P.G.T. Beauregard, later one of the most famous generals of the Confederacy, was stationed at Fort Pickens during its early years. Might we not surmise that he and the Barkleys were acquainted in the small nucleus of Pensacola citizenry? In 1861 Beauregard had climbed the ladder of promotion to be named as superintendent of the US Military Academy at West Point, only to resign from the US Army in early1862 in order to take a leading role in training and building up Confederate forces. General Pierre Gustave Toussaint Beauregard commanded the attack on Fort Sumter in South Carolina starting the Civil War. Had the possibility of Civil War been discussed at the Barkley House years before? As a young officer this historic figure was in all likelihood a guest at Pensacola's Barkley House. History, once again, on the Barkley doorstep.

George Walton II was secretary of the Florida Territory during the administration of Andrew Jackson. He was the son of Georgia governor George Walton I, a signer of the Declaration of Independence. It is a virtual certainty that in tiny territorial Pensacola, with the Walton house just around the corner, the Waltons and Barkleys were friends. The childhood relationship of his daughter Octavia to the Barkley's has been previously detailed.

Next, in 1822 William P. DuVal was appointed governor of the Florida Territory, at a time the capitol was located in Pensacola and when Barkley was well known in the tiny city. It would be a near certainty that they had extensive interaction, though this was too early for it to have been at the Barkley House.

A later governor, Richard Keith Call, governor of the Florida Territory from 1836 until removed from office in 1839 by President Van Buren, was an old Pensacolian, renowned for his "cavalry charge" up Palafox hill during a skirmish with the Seminoles. Because these were the glory days of the Barkleys in Pensacola, a relationship between the two must be inferred from their positions of prominence and the small size of the city. Call was reappointed as governor again in 1841 when William Henry Harrison defeated Van Buren, and continued to serve as governor until John Branch's appointment in 1844. Governor Call also served as territorial representative to the US Congress, where he was serving when he influenced Prince Achille Murat to seek fame and fortune in the wild new Florida Territory.

No doubt too George and Clara Barkley were well acquainted with Doctor A. P. Merrill, one of the frontier town's first medical doctors, appointed to the Pensacola Board of Health by Andrew Jackson in 1821 while Jackson served as acting governor of the territory.

While many Spanish residents melted away as the era of Spanish occupation ended in 1821, several remained and climbed the ladder of success under American rule. One such man was the esteemed Don Francisco Moreno, who served the young city admirably as both a banker and as Spanish Consul. Is it not logical that he and fellow banker George Barkley were colleagues?

With George Barkley's leadership in commerce, finance, and city administration, he would surely have made the acquaintance of the leaders at the "new" Pensacola Navy Yard. The destinies of Pensacola and the United States Navy were as intertwined then as they are now and ever have been; the whole greater than the sum of the parts. We have already noted Barkley's relationship with Andrew Jackson's agent at the Navy Yard, Byrd Charles Willis, but there was surely a collegial relationship among all of the top echelon of the Pensacola Navy Yard. Likely friends and associates of the Barkleys would have included the first commandant of the Pensacola Navy Yard, Commodore Warrington and it's second commander, Commodore A. J. Dallas, who married one of the Willis girls.

On the occasion of the visit by Bishop Kemper for the dedication of Christ Church, no doubt George Barkley, a founding warden, would have spent time with him. Perhaps the Barkleys even hosted Bishop Kemper at their new home by the bay, for it was just a few months old and the finest residence in the city.

As pivotal as George Barkley was in the young city of Pensacola, and as important as his large masonry home was, one can posit that virtually every important historic character in the development of the port city interacted with him, with a high likelihood that the historic Barkley House was the scene of the action. From 1820 until his death in 1854, the cast of characters surrounding George Barkley and the Barkley House reads like a history of Pensacola itself! Many Barkley associates are memorialized today with geographic landmarks and street names familiar to all northwest Floridians; Innerarity Point, Garnier Bayou, Brosnaham Park, Fort Walton, Jackson Street, LaRua Street, Gadsden Street, Chase Street and more; each a legacy of early Pensacola and each a colleague of George Barkley.

George Barkley's Father-in-Law John Garnier Struggles and Declines. Despairing for the restoration of a sympathetic ruler of France who would have allowed his return to France and recoupment of lost fortunes and positions in the aristocracy, John Garnier, Sr. continued to struggle in the unfamiliar environs of America's austere southern frontier. Business after business failed; timber, auctioneering, political appointments as Justice of the Peace, even a hotel on South Palafox Street. Appearing in the Pensacola *Gazette* of May 21, 1828 is this announcement.

Commercial Hotel

This house, lately occupied by Major Thomas Wright, was opened on the 6th of February by the subscriber, who respectfully solicits a share of the patronage of the public. All, which the localities afford, shall be studiously provided, and every attention devoted to the quiet and comfort of those who will favour the house with a preference.

An excellent billiard table, attached to the establishment occupying a separate building will contribute to the amusement without interfering with the good order and quiet of the House, and private parties can be always accommodated with a distinct sitting room.

There is on the premises one of the best stables in the place, where horses shall be strictly attended to.

John Garnier.

Alas, the enterprise was doomed and Garnier forced to "throw in the keys" without realizing the anticipated profit. It was only one of many such ill-fated efforts of the refugee aristocrat to adapt to the harsh realities of life as a commoner in a foreign land.

Despite his daughter Clara's well-to-do status as the wife of the wealthy George Barkley, the elder Garnier fell into poverty and depression, relying on the kindnesses of others, notably his son-in-law George Barkley, for the essentials of life.

Barkley was merely returning to his father-in-law the favors extended him by members of the Garnier family. Early Pensacola Deed Books provide evidence that Charles Garnier frequently extended credit to George W. Barkley, his brother in law. In turn, there are countless documented examples of Barkley's efforts to aid his father-in-law, the aging John Garnier, often working through Charles. It was a reciprocal, *quid pro quo* relationship, woven of both familial and business interests and the need to carve out a small personal slice of northwest Florida.

As relations between the Garniers and Barkleys matured, sealed by the marriage of Clara and George, it is evident that the esteem between the elder Garnier and George Barkley grew as well, and they continued to aid each other through difficult times. The records are replete with examples of Barkley's assistance to his father-in-law, the aging exile John Garnier. There were several loans between the two, as well as assistance finding gainful employment. The *Territorial Papers of the United States for the Territory of Florida* disclose that on April 1, 1826 George W. Barkley appointed John Garnier temporary tax collector and later as Inspector of Live Oaks at St. Andrews Bay to stop the decimation of valuable trees from federal lands. The destruction of public timber by unauthorized cutters was a serious problem on the southern frontier, and in this move, George Barkley both sought to ameliorate a real problem as well as give a financial boost to his father-in-law. It was a well-intentioned effort by Barkley, but a far cry from the status, wealth, and luxury to which the French aristocrat Garnier was accustomed.

Still later, we find another doomed business venture of the elder Garnier advertised in the Pensacola *Gazette*. The issue of October 10, 1833 carries the following:

LUMBER YARD
at Pensacola

The subscriber having selected an eligible situation within a short distance from the business part of the city for a LUMBER YARD, will always be ready to purchase, at cash prices, or to make liberal advances on lumber lands on account of owners, when preferred, and every exertion used to effect speedy and favorable sales. Orders from abroad from shippers and builders are solicited, and shall be attended to with dispatch and fidelity. Many mills, lately erected on tide water, render a constant supply at market, and the prompt execution of any orders for every description of lumber.

The highest cash price given for shingles.
John Garnier and Co.

Father of Clara Garnier Barkley and a refugee of high
status from France, John Garnier committed suicide in
Pensacola by drowning himself in the bay at Barkley Wharf,
sea-ward of today's Barkley House.

He is buried in St. Michael's Cemetery in a simple, almost
anonymous grave, a far cry from the glittering courts of
France he had known as a young man. His weathered stone
reads simply "John Garnier, a native of France, aged 81".
A victim of culture shock, the aristocratic Garnier never
succeeded as a commoner in the new world.

John Garnier's Suicide. The father of Clara Garnier Barkley, John Garnier, Sr., eternally hoped for eventual return to France and restoration of his privileged status. These hopes, however, were dashed when the aging Garnier waited in vain throughout the 1830's and 40's to be summoned back to France. Garnier colleague Prince Achille Murat, who had also longed for return to continental glories, had by this time died in Tallahassee, alcoholic, disspirited and discouraged, never to realize his dream of a Bonaparte resurgence or even to recoup his last fortunes.

Just as the Emperor of France had rewarded Princess Catherine Willis Murat with a generous stipend, John Garnier had relied on a similar financing from an unknown source in post-revolutionary France. We speculate that it was compensation for his confiscated fortune and lands. Without explanation, his stipend ceased, and in Pensacola the elder Garnier fell into poverty and lost what was left of his self-esteem. Still struggling with perpetually unsuccessful commercial ventures in Pensacola even into his very advanced age, (now about 78) we find in the Pensacola *Gazette* of Dec 30, 1843 an entry by John Garnier advertising a shipment of coffee from Cuba for sale.

Age, poverty after his French income stopped, declining health, and eventually unbearable despair gripped the aging Garnier. Each day, it is written, he would walk to the foot of Barkley Wharf on the bay in front of the Barkley House, scanning the horizon as if for news from home, returning in solitude to his diminished life in Pensacola ... a victim of the political upheavals of his native France ... and now penniless and shut out by the vicissitudes of ever-turbulent French politics. John Garnier's depression eventually got he better of him and the exiled French aristocrat, father of the Barkley House's first lady, at age 81 and afflicted with failing health, committed suicide by throwing himself into the bay at Barkley Wharf.

As his royal countryman Achille Murat was buried in Tallahassee, the self-exiled French aristocrat John Garnier was laid to final rest beneath the rich soil of his home-in-exile, Pensacola, Florida. John Garnier is buried in Pensacola's St. Michael's cemetery, with a simple marker reading cryptically, "John Garnier, a native of France, aged 81". At the very bottom of the stone is the inscription "J. Stroud and Co., N.O.", suggesting that the stone was ordered by his sons John, Jr. and Charles, of New Orleans. His burial is opposite the Barkley plot at Pensacola's St. Michael's cemetery while Prince Murat's grave is in St. John's Cemetery in Tallahassee, where he was joined years later by his wife Kate, wife of the Crown Prince of Naples and the two Sicilies and a Princess of France's Second Empire in her own right; the daughter of Pensacola Brickmaker Byrd Charles Willis; George Barkley's business colleague and in-law.

Prince Murat's epitaph reads "Departed this life April 18, 1847, Charles Louis Napoleon Achille Murat, son of King of Naples and Caroline Murat. This monument is dedicated by his wife Catherine in perpetual memory of her love.

Alongside, on a matching shaft, "Princess Kate's" epitaph reads. "Sacred to the memory of Princess C. D. Murat, widow of Col. (NB: his title in the Florida militia) Charles Louis Napoleon Achille Murat, and daughter of the late Bird (sic) C. Willis of Virginia, who departed this life on the 6th of August, 1867 in the 64th year of her age. A kind and affectionate wife and sister, a sincere and devoted friend. None knew her but to love her; none named her but to praise. This monument is erected to her memory by her beloved brothers and sisters."

With their gravesite adorned with the royal coat of arms of the Murat family; thus ended the saga of Florida's prince and princess, each linked in a close web of relationships to Pensacola's Garnier, Barkley, Willis, and Call families; another vignette of Pensacola history spun in part at the historic Barkley House.

The Barkley Family on the Florida Frontier. George and Clara Barkley following the custom of the day reared a large family. Honoring the nobility of their Garnier blood, five of their nine children had the middle name of Garnier. Other commonly used Garnier given names are perpetuated by the Barkley children; Charles, Rosa, Sophia (Sophie), and Adeline. Four of the Barkley children were born before the assumed date of construction of the Barkley House, while five were most likely born within it's walls.

The Barkley children, in order of date of birth, were:

George Garnier Barkley
Born April 29, 1823
Died June 29, 1858

George Garnier Barkley never married, and is buried in St. Michaels Cemetery,

The pride with which the Garnier name was carried from France to America is seen in its perpetuation in the names of the children born to George and Clara Garnier Barkley. The St. Michael's Cemetery grave of George Garnier Barkley is but one example.

Clara Garnier Barkley
Born 1825
Died 1899

Married(1) Noel Armande Vienne, September 15, 1840
(2) Eben Walker Dorr, December 2, 1849

The fate of the original grave marker of Clara Garnier Barkley is not known, but a later generation of Clara Barkley's descendants, the Vienne family of New Orleans, placed this marker at St. Michael's Cemetery, where countless prominent early Pensacolians are interred. The final resting place in Pensacola of this childhood refugee from political turmoil in France is a poignant end to her saga and an important chapter of Pensacola history. RIP.

Clara married Eben Dorr, a prominent timber tycoon of Bagdad, Florida and son of Ebenezer Dorr, a "downeast" sea captain who moved to Pensacola from his home in Maine. Clara Barkley Dorr's husband Eben was the Territorial Sheriff when Jonathan Walker's hand was branded for stealing the slaves of George Willis, giving rise to Whittier's poem, *"The Branded Hand"*. After her husband's death, Clara Barkley Dorr built the historic Dorr House at 311 Adams Street on Seville Square in Pensacola, another prized historic landmark.

Clara Garnier Barkley married Eben Dorr, son of Maine sea captain Ebenezer Dorr and a timber tycoon in nearby Bagdad. After her husband's death, Clara Barkley Dorr built another of Pensacola's most historic homes, the Dorr House, which in 2005 was the home of the president of the University of West Florida.

Another of Pensacola's historic jewels is the Dorr House, fronting Seville Square. George and Clara Barkley's daughter Clara Garnier Barkley married Eben Dorr, originally of Augusta, Maine, and a timber tycoon from neighboring Bagdad, FL. After his death in 1870, the widowed Clara built this icon of Pensacola history, which in 2005 was the home of the president of the University of West Florida. The Dorr House and the Barkley House, both National Registry properties, are thus "related by marriage"!

Charles Garnier Barkley
Born 1826
Date of death unknown, in Texas.

He was named for Clara Barkley's older brother who practiced law in New Orleans with Prince Achille Murat.

Rosa Garnier Barkley
Born ca. February 18, 1828
Died in childhood March 18, 1831

Rosa was named for Clara Garnier Barkley's sister, Rosa Garnier. In the Barkley plot in St Michael's cemetery Pensacola is this haunting epitaph on the gravestone of three-year-old Rosa. It was placed by tearful parents George and Clara who would later bury yet another daughter in infancy.

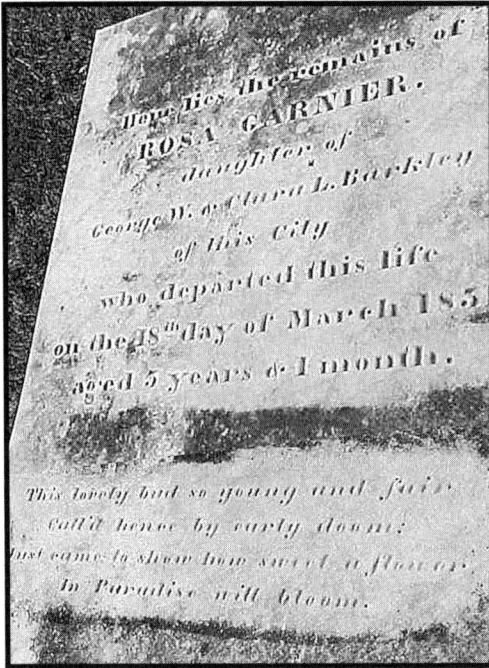

Rosa Garnier Barkley's gravestone and the poem underneath which reads:

"This lovely bird so young and fair
Called hence by early doom
Just came to show how sweet a flower
In Paradise will bloom".

Lucy Rose Barkley
Born January 9, 1831
Died 1865/66

Lucy Rose Barkley married Byrd Charles Willis II October 12, 1854 at Christ Church, where she had served as organist and music director for many years. The Pensacola *Gazette* of October 14, 1854 carries the notice *"Married in this city on Thursday evening last, at the Episcopal Church, by the Rev. J.J. Scott, Mr. Byrd C. Willis to Miss Lucy Rose, second daughter of the late George W. Barkley, Esq."* In the records of Christ Church for 1854 is the entry *"Charles Byrd Willis (sic) to Lucy Rose Barkley. The bride is a communicant and served the church faithfully as an organist for 14 years previous to her marriage."* She had been also the very first child Christened there after the original dedication of the church. Early photos of Lucy Rose Barkley and Byrd Charles Willis II are found on page 81. More details follow in later pages.

Adeline Garnier Barkley
Born August 14, 1838
Date of death is unknown.

Re-interred in St. Michaels Cemetery April 30, 1867, her first burial site was likely out of the city during a yellow fever epidemic. Adeline Garnier Barkley never married. She was named for the first wife of John Garnier, Clara Barkley's father in law. The Adeline Garnier for whom Adeline Garnier Barkley was named passed away in France before John Garnier immigrated to the United States. Another Adeline Garnier was born to immigrant Bordeaux-born John Garnier and his American wife Ann in memory of his deceased first French wife.

The Christening cups of two of the daughters of George and Clara Barkley; Lucy Rose and Adeline. Over 175 years old, Lucy Rose's cup helped identify her date of birth. She was the first child Christened in "Old Christ Church" on Pensacola's Seville Square, the oldest church in Florida.

Lucy Rose Barkley   *Adeline Garnier Barkley*

Sophie Elizabeth Barkley
Born ca. 1834
Died May 24, 1901

Named for the wife of Charles Garnier, Clara's brother who remained in New Orleans. Sophie married Enoch Sawyer May 13, 1852 at Trinity Episcopal Church in Mobile, where they settled. Sophie and Enoch eloped by boat from in front of the Barkley House and, never forgiven by her stern father George Barkley, as a result of his displeasure at her elopement, he left her the customary $1 as a sign of his displeasure. After her father's death in 1854, Sophie and her mother, Clara Barkley, enjoyed a reconciliation with her mother and siblings and was once again welcomed at the Barkley House.

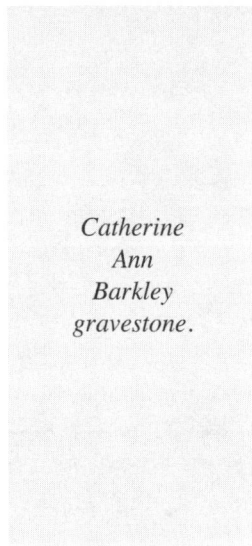

*Catherine
Ann
Barkley
gravestone.*

Catherine Ann Barkley
Born December 16, 1835
Died in infancy June 18, 1836

It is believed that Catherine was named for Catherine Willis Murat; "Princess Kate", as the name Catherine is not common within either the Garnier or Barkley families. Catherine Willis Murat, "Princess Kate", was at the peak of her fame in 1835, at a time when business and social relations between George Barkley and Catherine Willis Murat's father, Byrd Charles Willis were at their apex. As has been noted, the Willis and Barkley families enjoyed a special and close relationship. Naming a daughter thusly would have been a mark of special respect and closeness, and a nod to the international reknown of this famed family friend. Tragically Catherine was another Barkley child to die young. Catherine and Rosa Barkley <u>both</u> died in early childhood and both are buried in a common raised grave in St. Michaels Cemetery.

Margaret Overton Barkley
Born August 14, 1838, the twin of Adeline Garnier Barkley

Married Alfred Francis Vienne August 8, 1857, she was known to the family as Margie.

George Barkley Helps Found Pensacola's Venerable Christ Church.
We make an informed assumption that English born George Barkley was a member of the Church of England before his lifetime sojourn to the United States. When he settled down in the small and still primitive military outpost of Pensacola, he would have felt deprived of the familiar liturgy of the church of his childhood in England. In the 1820's in Pensacola, still very much a Spanish oriented community, "the church" meant the Roman Catholic Church, and that faith dominated the city's landscape. Prior to the change of flags in 1821, under Catholic Spain, it was the only Church authorized, though there had been a small Protestant congregation which met at various sites around town. Together with other influential young business and political leaders, Barkley saw the need for a Protestant church in his adopted hometown of Pensacola. Support for a new protestant church was enhanced by Andrew Jackson's wife Rachel, who expressed shock and dismay at the bawdy waterfront life of the seaport town. Rachel *prayed and prayed that a minister of the Gospel would come over to help the Lord."*

As a founding warden of Christ Church, George Barkley was instrumental in the details of its construction as well as its founding. Former Rector of Christ Church, Dr. B. Madison Currin has done extensive research on the early church, and has published three books on the subject. During conversation with Dr. Currin in January, 2001, the author was advised that the brick for the "Old Christ Church" on Seville Square had been provided by George W. Barkley. But Barkley had no brickyard, and this set in motion another round of historic sleuthing. Where did the materials for Christ Church come from? The following scenario is now believed plausible.

When the church was authorized to be built in 1829, one of George Barkley's colleagues was the Colonel Byrd Charles Willis described previously. Willis and Henry Slayback <u>did</u> have a brickyard, and the B.C. Willis Brickyard employed Barkley's ships to transport their brick. The Barkley and Willis families would soon be joined in intermarriage; Byrd Charles Willis II to Barkley daughter Lucy Rose. Willis, late of Virginia had been raised in the staunchly Episcopal aristocracy of Virginia, and like Barkley was eager to see the construction of a familiar house of worship in his adopted hometown of Pensacola. We know from multiple sources that Barkley <u>delivered</u> the brick for construction of Old Christ Church in 1831, but in all likelihood they were actually Willis brick, <u>transported</u> by Barkley's vessels. Pensacola Historical Society officials affirm that "Willis brick" has been found at the Old Christ Church site, and one is in possession of the author's family, strengthening the circumstantial case for the above theory.

George W. Barkley, builder of Pensacola's historic Barkley House, was a founding warden of Christ Church and Barkley descendants have been active parishioners for many generations, until this very day. "Old" Christ Church is a crown jewel of early Pensacola architecture and some believe it to have been designed by Sir Christopher Wren. Today it stands proudly beside historic Seville Square, the oldest church in Florida. (Image courtesy of Pensacola Historical Society).

There are records that John Garnier's American-born wife Ann and their daughter Adeline joined the Barkleys in their commitment to the church. One of their outreach projects was a meeting at the Navy Yard to consider the creation of a church in that western "suburb" of Pensacola, Warrington. On the board of the new church, St. Johns, was J. W. Shippey, whom Adeline Garnier married.

Barkley Descendants and Antecedents. One could fill several volumes tracing the descendants of the Barkleys, however that is not the purpose of this book. This book seeks rather to focus on those known persons and events of historical significance at the time George and Clara occupied their famous home by the bay. One exception is made to this general criteria for the book. The marriage of one of the Barkley daughters is uniquely significant, in that she married a Washington descendant, thereby linking Pensacola's Barkley name with that most famous of American names and to the European royalty from whom the Washington family descends.

Lucy Rose Barkley's Marriage Links the Family to Royalty; the Second Willis Family Connection. It was to fall to the daughter of George and Clara Barkley, young Lucy Rose Barkley, to cement the family's links with George Washington and with a vast panoply of European royalty dating to the Emperor Charlemagne and earlier. The key would be in her marriage also into the Willis family of Virginia, and later of Pensacola, the same family which had intermarried with Napoleon's nephew, Prince Achille Murat.

The musical Lucy Rose Barkley, who served as music director of Old Christ Church, was the second daughter of the family of nine Barkley children. It was especially significant for her father George Barkley when Lucy Rose was the first child Christened in Christ Church; the church he had worked so tirelessly to establish.

Lucy Rose Barkley's young life was filled with both the simple childhood pleasures of the era beside the shores of Pensacola Bay, as well as with training in the social graces by her elegant French mother. No doubt Clara Garnier Barkley tutored young Lucy Rose in a genteel style more akin to her native France than to the rough-and-tumble atmosphere of early Pensacola, and this training would later serve her well in her marriage into one of Pensacola's distinguished aristocratic families, the Willises. We may surmise that under the tutelage of her Bordeaux-born mother Clara Garnier Barkley, Lucy Rose spoke French as well as her native English.

In this environment, it is certain that Lucy Rose Barkley matured through the 1830's and 40's into an accomplished and sophisticated young lady. In addition to her social graces, achievements in music, and her devotion to Christ Church, Lucy Rose was reputedly an articulate conversationalist and forceful yet ladylike advocate of her views on a wide range of topics.

As leaders of the community, George and Clara Barkley were surely on the lookout for likely marriage prospects for their daughters. In the person of Byrd Charles Willis II (grandson of Virginia-born Pensacola resident, Colonel Byrd Charles Willis, Barkley's business associate) a likely candidate was found. Their romance flourished through the hot summer of 1854, taking a poignantly sad turn when Lucy Rose's father, George W. Barkley died that August, at the virtual peak of their courtship. Shortly after her George Barkley's death, on October 12, 1854 Lucy Rose Barkley and the aristocratic Willis, close heir to the dynasty of George Washington, joined in matrimony before the historic altar of the very church her father had energetically supported as a founder, vestryman, and warden, Christ Episcopal Church, close by the Barkley House. There on Seville Square it still stands proudly, the oldest church in Florida and yet another priceless treasure of Pensacola's past. There, too Lucy Rose had been the first child Christened in the then-new sanctuary, and where she had lovingly and faithfully served as music director and organist for sixteen years. Sadly, her father was no longer living to share this happiest of days when she married into the Washington family via Byrd Charles Willis II.

The notice of their marriage appeared in the Pensacola *Gazette* of October 14, 1854. "*Married in this city on Thursday evening last, at the Episcopal Church (Old Christ Church), by the Rev. J.J. Scott, Mr. Byrd Charles Willis to Miss Lucy Rose, second daughter of the late George W. Barkley, Esq.*" After their marriage, they resided at 412 Zaragossa Street, near the Barkley homestead at 410 Florida Blanca. Their photographs in old age appear on page 81.

Lucy Rose Barkley Willis. One could fill volumes with the lineage this marriage created. Suffice to say it gave to their descendants the direct link to the family of George Washington, thence back in time to many of the kings and queens of England, France, Spain, the Scandinavian countries and to other notables such as a number of the Magna Charta surety barons. Even the illustrious Emperor Charlemagne, founder of the Holy Roman Empire, is found in their pedigree. This lineage now belongs to Pensacola for all time.

The Decline and Death of George W. Barkley. Customs inspector, auctioneer, prosperous merchant, bank president, by reputation "the richest man in Pensacola", co-founder of Christ Church, city official of the territorial period, officer of the 1st Brigade Florida Militia, and the English gentleman ever, George Barkley was generous to a fault with family and friend alike. In later life he endorsed the bond of a U.S. Marshal, who defaulted, costing the Barkleys much of their fortune. Widow Clara struggled to pay the indebtedness, but pay it she did.

At the time of George Barkley's death on a sweltering afternoon in August 1854, George Barkley's fortunes had already diminished significantly, but he had by this time lent the Barkley genes to later generations who would continue his good works, and his place in the history of early Pensacola was already assured. At Christ Church under records of funerals is found the following entry. "*August 9, 1854 - George W. Barkley, a native of England but an old resident and identified with the early history of the Parish. He has been a vestryman and warden and at the time of his death, a communicant.*" George W. Barkley was laid to final rest in St. Michael's Roman Catholic cemetery which was still the preferred location for burials and referred to by Barkley in his will as "*the burying ground of the City of Pensacola.*"

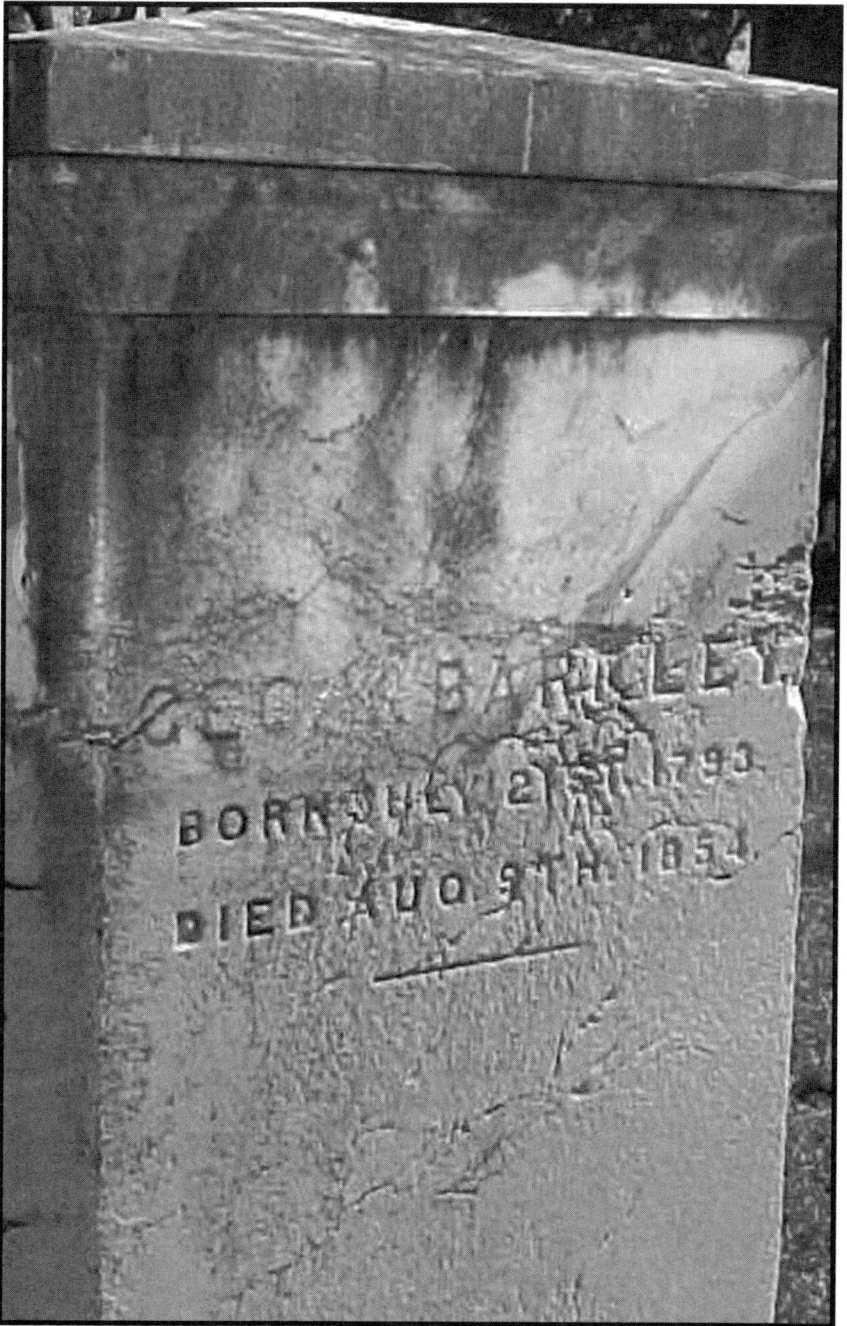

George W. Barkley, born July 25, 1793 in London, was one of early Pensacola's most prominent businessmen and leaders. Much of the early history of the city played out at his home which we know today as the national registry Barkley House. George Barkley died in August 1854 and is buried in St. Michael's Cemetery.

Court records of the next few years are filled with various notices regarding disposition of the various parts of George W. Barkley's estate. Tragically for his widow Clara, the United States government moved against the estate to recover the defaulted surety bond monies mentioned above, and we find an entry dated May 8th, 1860. *"Pensacola. $250 received of Charles G. Barkley as executor of the estate of George W. Barkley. Two Hundred and Fifty Dollars for professional services rendered in the case of U.S. vs. Executors of Land of George W. Barkley."*

The eulogy of George Barkley found in the August 12, 1854 Pensacola *Gazette* synopsizes his reputation. *"As a citizen he was ever ready to accord his influence and means for the promotion of public morals, the diffusion of education, and the relief and comfort of the poor and needy. He was an exemplary member of the Episcopal Church (NB: Christ Church, which he helped to found.) and very strict in the observance of all his duties as such."*

Late in life, with the previous Barkley fortunes dissipated, French born aristocrat Clara Garnier Barkley fell victim to the yellow fever epidemic of 1867, succumbing finally at the end of August at age 67. It would be almost thirty years until medical science would link the scourge of yellow fever to the ubiquitous mosquitos of Pensacola!

Like her father, husband, and five of their nine children, Clara Garnier Barkley is buried in St Michael's cemetery, with a recent vintage headstone placed by a descendant through the Vienne line.

The Past is Prologue. We have seen how two immigrant families of Barkley and Garnier made their way to Pensacola during the last days of Spanish rule, and how their alliance forged an important foundation for the later growth of the city of Pensacola. With much fact and written record, filled in with informed speculation, we have cobbled together a historical vignette of George W. Barkley, his family, and the amazing cast of characters who likely enjoyed the hospitality of Pensacola's revered Barkley House, now owned by the state and, as a part of Historic Pensacola Village, on the National Registry of Historic Places.

We have examined scraps of evidence and attempted to create from them a humanized glimpse of the lives of George and Clara Barkley, and those of their associates in the exciting, yet difficult, days of Pensacola following the Spanish occupation. We have joined them in sadness as Clara's father took his own life and when they followed the small caskets of two of their children to St. Michael's cemetery, gone too soon. We mentally heard their voices lifted in song in their beloved Christ Church, which they had been instrumental in founding when it was consecrated in 1838. We rejoiced with them in Christ Church at Christenings and the weddings of their accomplished children. We have laughed with them over French wines brought by the Garniers from New Orleans, conspired with them and perhaps the nephew of Napoleon to recoup lost French fortunes and titles. We have eavesdropped on their conversations with princes, governors, congressmen, mayors, and distinguished authors on endless topics ranging from slavery to duels to yellow fever to what bonnet to wear to the dedication of Christ Church; Florida's oldest church. We whooped with glee with them when Florida was admitted as the 27th state of the union, offering the unlimited promise provided by the U.S. Constitution. We dealt with carriages stuck in the sand, with scratchy wool suits, cock roaches and cock fights, lawsuits, duels, and more; through good times and bad. We have laughed and cried with them; lived and died with them, and we have tried to see their essential human-ness through the dark glass of an incomplete historical record. Despite the fragmentary evidence for the preceding work, this story of the Barkleys and their house is not historical fiction. It is the best-available historical fact extrapolated to fill in the blanks with reasoned and logical linkages and it sheds realistic light on some of the most important families and events in territorial Pensacola.

These have been vignettes of Pensacola history associated with our most historic property, the Barkley House, and tales of the fascinating characters who populated the port city; the very people who created the city we know and love.

Their past is the strong foundation of our present. May our contributions to the dynamic city that is Pensacola be as great.

APPENDIX 1

Extract of the origins of the Barkley House by Historic Pensacola Preservation Board, 1984. (Note: The work of the Historic Preservation Board is now under the aegis of West Florida Historic Preservation, Inc.)

Why is the Barkley house so important? And what is the history of this fascinating old building? As is true of many of Pensacola's buildings, these questions are difficult to answer because of the great age of the building as well as the many stories, legends, and half-truths which over the years have become associated with it. The Barkley house is the oldest standing masonry building in the city of Pensacola. Unfortunately, beyond this statement, the history of the building is subject to intense and highly emotional debate. The date of the construction of the Barkley house cannot yet be established with total accuracy. Some Pensacolians insist that the building is of British or Spanish origin, which would make it among the oldest, if not the oldest, building in Pensacola. Several arguments are advanced for a colonial origin for the Barkley house, and each has its flaws.

First, there is tradition. According to some, the Barkley house was originally the Spanish garrison house. Others insist on an English origin for the house which, they say, could have been associated with an English redoubt built in 1779 near the end of what is Zaragoza Street today. These legends and traditions, however, are in direct conflict which holds that George Barkley, and English merchant, constructed the house. According to Pensacola historian Leora Sutton, Barkley did not arrive in Pensacola until 1821, after Florida was transferred from Spain to the United States. Obviously, the tradition surrounding the date of construction of the Barkley house are mutually exclusive and cannot all be true.

Architectural evidence is frequently cited to support a colonial date for the Barkley house. The "colonialists" quite correctly point out that the architectural style of the Barkley house was popular during the second Spanish period. The house in many ways resembles the Creole cottage brought to Pensacola from the French Gulf Coast colonies of the eighteenth century. The building is a single-gable, one and one-half story raised brick cottage. The brick exterior of the building is stuccoed and scored to resemble stone. Three dormers open onto the east and west slopes of the roof. Originally, the building had a recessed porch on the east side and a two-tiered wrap-around porch on the west and south sides. Superficially, the building probably resembled the Tivoli high house, when it was constructed. However, this does not necessarily mean that the Barkley house dates to the second Spanish period. Creole cottages remained popular and continued to be constructed well into the 1880s. One detail of the Barkley house's design which may provide a clue about the builder has generally been over looked. The building has chimneys at the gable ends, a feature which is typical of Creole cottages but characteristic of Georgian and Federal architecture. Barkley, a native Englishman, and a merchant who travelled fairly extensively, would have had exposure to these architectural styles. It is possible that Barkley attempted to emulate other architectural styles while retaining the functional climatic advantages of the Creole cottage.

One further place of evidence which can be said to argue for a colonial date of construction is found in the east wall of the Barkley house basement. The lower courses of this wall consist of larger than standard sized brick of indisputably Spanish origin. However, once again, the appearance of such brick does not necessarily mean that those brick were laid during the second Spanish period. If Barkley did indeed build the house between 1821 and 1835, he would, of course, have needed a supply of brick. Most of the brick manufactured in the Pensacola area during this period was earmarked for military or commercial construction, hence Barkley may have had difficulty securing the brick he needed. The practice of salvaging bricks from older buildings was well established. Archeological evidence uncovered by Dr. Bense suggests that Barkley may indeed have used salvaged bricks. Several British brick which had been cleaned and re-mortared were found in one of the piers which once supported the Barkley's cook's house.

Additional evidence can be mustered to debunk a colonial date for the Barkley house. While British and second Spanish period maps show buildings near the site of the Barkley house, none show a building exactly corresponding to it. Leora Sutton, in her work on the Barkley house, cites an 1804 deed for Lot 31, Old City Tract, (the Barkley house lot) which states that a wooden house stood on the property at that date. This is also supported by the recent archaeology excavation behind the Barkley house, which unearthed a log sill. Artifacts found in association with this foundation make a second Spanish period date highly likely. It is highly unlikely, given the proximity of this building to the east side of the Barkley house that they co-existed.

Given the weight of evidence arguing against a colonial origin for the Barkley house, it seems highly likely that the merchant and attorney, George Barkley, constructed the house in the early years of the Territorial period. Once again, it is impossible at this time to assign an exact date of construction to the house, though further research may indeed uncover it one day. Barkley acquired lot 31 in 1825 for $500. However, the house is located almost on the south line of the lot. It seems unlikely that he would construct so large a house, with its overhanging southern porch, so close to the lot line unless he also owned lot 25, the adjacent lot to the south. This he purchased in 1835. However, one final problem sheds some doubt on the 1835 construction date. Lot 25 was purchased in 1827 by Charles Garnier, Barkley's brother-in-law, and client. It is certainly possible that Barkley constructed the house while Garnier owned the adjacent property.

This article is not intended to disparage the colorful legends which surround the Barkley house, but rather to show the careful research from varied sources which must be performed in order to accurately establish the construction date of early Pensacola buildings. Evidence from deeds, documents, architecture and the archaeological record help the historian to establish the origin of the Barkley house. While the weight of evidence seems to support a construction date in the first two decades of the Territorial period, the importance of the Barkley house as an historic site and cultural artifact is not diminished. Barkley was one of the most prominent merchants of the Territorial period, and his descendants continued to play an active role in the growth of Pensacola well into the twentieth century. As the oldest masonry building in the city of Pensacola, it serves as a tribute and reminder of George Barkley and the early years of Pensacola's growth under the American republic.

Summary of the Archaeological Fieldwork for the Barkley House Restoration Project; Dr. Judith A. Bense; Archaeology Institute, The University of West Florida. Fieldwork December 1983; report 1984. The author gratefully acknowledges the permission of Dr. Bense to reproduce this summary of her field notes in their entirety.

Fieldwork has been completed for the Barkley House Restoration Project. Archaeological services were conducted between December the 19, 1983 and January 2, 1984 under the direct supervision of Dr. Judith A. Bense. The results of the fieldwork will allow accurate reconstruction of the structure and attached buildings. All work was monitored by the Historic Pensacola Preservation Board and the project architect, Mr. Larry Barrow. While laboratory work is just beginning, below is a summary of the archaeological information which was recovered. Enclosed is a map of all features encountered at the Barkley House for reference in this summary. It should be noted that some interpretation of the features could change with laboratory analysis and research of the recovered materials.

A total of 22 features were encountered in the five trenches opened for investigation. The trenches were placed in reference to the architectural reconstruction drawings by Mr. Barrow. Of the 22 features discovered, 12 were architectural and related to the Barkley House. One additional foundation pier may be also associated with the house. One architectural feature of a previous structure probably built in the 18th century was also encountered. The remaining features were typical residential features such as refuse pits, piles and dark stains.

The Barkley House features which can be identified with the original structure are as follows:

Kitchen: located the northeast corner pier (Feature 3) and the chimney (Feature 5). The pier was in excellent shape with three courses remaining, however the chimney had been somewhat disturbed with only the eastern side remaining with two courses.

The south wall and walkway piers were not present. Trench III was placed in this area and none were recovered.

The dimensions of the kitchen are 22x16 feet.

South Porch: located two piers (Features 9 and 10) and one pit where the pier had been removed (Features 9 and 10) and one pit where the pier had been removed (Feature 14). The two intact piers were well preserved, had three courses of bricks were 2.5 feet square. Both has been placed on a prepared base of white sand. The removed pier had a few brick fragments remaining and a definite shovel-dug pit associated with it.

The porch was 10 feet wide with foundation piers on 11.5 to 12.0 foot centers and ran the length of the house (46 feet).

West Porch: two of the foundation piers were preserved (Features 17 and 18) and one had been removed with fragments remaining (Feature 22). The two piers were made of very different brick, and Feature 17 appears to have been younger and was constructed differently. Both are 2.5 feet square. The removed pier was in the correct position and the remaining brick fragments were of the original age of Feature 18.

The dimensions of the porch were 4 to 5 feet wide, piers which were 2.5 feet square and placed on 11.5 to 12.0 foot centers. These are the same dimensions and placing as the South porch indicating they were constructed at the same time.

Cooks House: This was the most poorly preserved structure. Only one foundation pier was located: the northwest corner (Feature 19). The south wall features were located, but all had been disturbed. These included the southwest corner (Feature 15), the southeast corner (Feature 21) and the chimney (Feature 16).

The northwest corner (Feature 19) was of an unusual size and shape. It was "T" shaped with the small portion of the same size as the Kitchen (1.5 feet square), however, the larger portion on the eastern side was 2.7 by 1.5 feet. There was one interlaced course (3rd) indicating construction at the same time. This is probably an extra-supported pier due perhaps to its position on the corner.

Even though there was some disturbance, the dimensions of the cook's house can be determined: 16 feet square with piers on eight foot centers.

Walkway: only two features of the walkway were located: The Cook's House northwest corner (Feature 19) and a pile of disturbed brick 8 feet north of it (Feature 20). These were the only remaining features encountered.

The only dimension of the walkway which can be suggested is that the piers appeared to be on 8 foot centers and it did connect with the kitchen.

There were a few other features encountered which will provide information concerning the Barkley house use. These include a refuse pit (Feature 12), a pile of refuse under the kitchen (Feature 4), and a refuse pit (Feature 11) under the South Porch. Analysis will be necessary for further information.

An interesting and highly unusual architectural feature was also encountered. This is a dirt sill of a wooden structure (Feature 8/13) which appears to have been constructed during the 18th century. The artifacts associated with it are from this time period and they appear to be in primary context. One pit (Feature 7) seems to be associated with this occupation of the property. Further research and analysis will be necessary to interpret these features, but it is the first wooden structure encountered in Pensacola from the 18th century.

In summary, the archaeological investigations for the Barkley House have been completed and were quite successful. Accurate dimensions and foundation positions can be documented for the Kitchen, South Porch and West Porch. The Cook's House can be well estimated and the walkway between the Kitchen and Cook's House can be also estimated. There were no major field problems except extreme cold and rainy weather conditions. It is unfortunate that the temperatures reached 8°, however, it did not effect the field work. We had excellent cooperation from the Historic Pensacola Preservation Board and William Graves architectural firm and the work went very smoothly.

BIBLIOGRAPHY

Life in Pensacola, by Clarence Edward Carter, Territorial Papers of the United States, V 22, pp 481-483, The Territory Florida 1824-1828, George Walton, Jr.

George Barkley, by Leora M. Sutton, a speech by Ms. Sutton now bound and found in the archives of the Pensacola Historical Society

The Walton House, by Leora M. Sutton, Pensacola 1968.

Escambia County Footprints (detailing 1845 Escambia County voters), by Sheila Martin and the West Florida Genealogical Society.

Clara Barkley — Facts and Speculation, from the files of the Pensacola Heritage Foundation, Inc.,

A Sketch of the Willis Family - Fredericksburg Branch, by Byrd Charles Willis, Whittet and Shepperson, Richmond, Virginia, 1909

The Willis Family of Virginia, by Adelaide Rutherford Willis, published by Paperwork, Mobile, AL; 1967

A Historical Guide to Pensacola, a brochure produced by the Pensacola Chamber of Commerce, Pensacola Historic Board, and the Bureau of Historic Preservation, Florida Department of State, Tallahassee

Historic Architecture of Pensacola, published by the Pensacola Historical, Restoration, and Preservation Commission, Pensacola, Florida ("Barkley House") NB: The work of this organization is now in the hands of the West Florida Preservation Board, an entity of the University of West Florida

Glimpses of Old Mobile, published by DuVal Printing Company, date unknown, ca 1930

Mobile of the Five Flags, by Peter J. Hamilton, LL.D., The Gill Printing Company, Mobile, Alabama,1913

A Prince in Their Midst, The Adventurous Life of Achille Murat on the American Frontier, by A. J. Hanna, University of Oklahoma Press, 1946

The Betrayers: Joachim and Caroline Murat, by Huber Cole, Eyre Methuen, London, 1972.

Napoleon and King Murat, by Albert Espitalier, translated from the French by J. Lewis May, John Lane Company, New York, MCMXII

Marshall Murat, by A. Hilliard Atteridge, Thomas Nelson and Sons Ltd, London, undated

Achille Murat en Belgique, by Maurice A. Arnould, University of Brussels Press, Brussels, 1938

Caroline Murat, by Joan Bear, Collins Publishers, St. James Place, London, 1972. ISBN 0-00-211186-1.

America and the Americans, by Achille Murat, George H. Derby and Company, Buffalo, 1851.

Napoleon: His Wives and Women, by Christopher Hibbert, Harper Collins Publishers, London, 2002, ISBN 0-00-257092-0

Madame LeVert, by Frances Gibson Satterfield, Edisto Press, Edisto Island, SC, ISBN 0-9618589-1-5,. 1987

Madame Octavia Walton LeVert: The South's Most Famous Belle. By Caldwell Delaney. Published by the Mobile Historic Preservation Society, 1961.

Florida During Territorial Days, by Sidney W. Martin, University of Georgia Press, Athens, GA, 1944. reprint; Porcupine Press, Philadelphia.

The Return of Lafayette 1824-1825, by Marian Klamkin. Charles Scribner and Sons, NY, 1975, ISBN 0-6841-3887-5

Napoleon III, A Life; by Fenton Bresler, Carroll and Graf Publishers, New York, 1999, ISBN 0-7867-0660-0

St. Michael's Cemetery 1807-?, by Lola Lee Daniell, 1938, for the National Society DAR Library, with additions of 1986

Various Archived Court Records located in the Judicial Center, City of Pensacola, Florida

"Rebuilding History in 400-Year Old Pensacola", an article by Wylly Folk St.John, in *The Atlanta Constitution,* May 5, 1958

"The Barkley House", article by B. Galman, in *Pensacola Bay Magazine*, January 1987

"Barkley House — Restoration Efforts Stress Authenticity", article by Helen Finnegan Pratt, in *Pensacola Bay Magazine*, June 1988

Eugenie and Napoleon III, by David Duff, William Morrow and Company, New York, 1978, ISBN 0-688-03338-5

Napoleon and the American Dream, by Ines Murat, copyright 1976 by Librairie Artheme Fayard, Paris; translation copyright 1981 by Louisiana State University Press, Baton Rouge and London, ISBN 0-8071-0770-0

Some Prominent Virginia Families, by Louise Pecquet du Bellet, Genealogical Publishing Company, Inc, Baltimore, 1976, originally published in Lynchburg, VA 1907. ISBN 0-8063-0722-6

Jonathan Walker; The Man With The Branded Hand, by Alvin F. Oickle 1998, ISBN 0-9664556-0-6, Lorelli Slater Publishing, Everett, MA 02149

"Pensacola in 1810", *Florida Historical Quarterly,* 32 (July 1953), page 45

Pensacola - The Old and the New — A Guide to Pensacola and Surrounding Areas, published by Pensacola Historical Society, ca 1988

Pamphlet "*Barkley House — A Marriage of Cultures*" published by the Pensacola Heritage Foundation, Pensacola, Florida

Jackson and the Enchanted City, Stories of Old Pensacola, by Celia Myrover Robinson

Pensacola - The Deep Water City, by Lucius and Linda Ellsworth, Continental Heritage Press, Tulsa, OK, Second Edition, 1982

Pensacola - Florida's First Place City - A Pictorial History, The Donning Company Publishers, Norfolk, VA., 1989, ISBN 0-89865-777-6

Christ Church Parish, Pensacola, Florida 1827-1927, by Julia J. Yonge

Territorial Papers of the United States, V22; The Territory of Florida, 1824-1828, George Walton, Jr, "Life in Pensacola", Florida Historical Quarterly, pp481-483

Escambia County Deed Books A, B, and C

Escambia County Will Books

Internet site of Clan Barclay. www.clanbarclay.com

From One Generation to Another, A History of Christ Church (Episcopal), Pensacola, Florida 1827-1903, by Beverly Madison Currin, Th.D, 1995

The Barkley House, by Leora M. Sutton, 1962 (updated 1979)

Pensacola Historic Landmarks, 4th Edition (revised), 1983, Pensacola Historic Preservation Society.

The Bonapartes in America, by Clarence Edward Macartney and Gordon Dorrance. Published: Philadelphia, Dorrance and company [c1939].

Princesse Achille Murat, a biographical sketch, by Mrs. Ellen Call Long, Florida. Published: Richmond, Virginia: The William Byrd Press, 1931.

Early French in North Florida, by Sudarsan Rangarajan and Evan Plaskett. Published: Tallahassee, Fla.: The Florida/France Linkage Institute, Florida State University, 1995.

Recollections of a Virginian in the Mexican, Indian, and Civil Wars, by General Dabney Herndon Maury. Second Edition, New York, Charles Scribner's Sons, 1894.

Petersburg (Virginia) *Index Appeal*, March 18, 1889.

The Pensacola *News Journal:*
   Nov 1, 1934
   June 30, 1959
   Nov 24, 1959
   August 23, 1961
   March 28, 1965
   February 19, 1967
   October 29, 1983
   January 5, 1984
   December 4, 1984
   January 7, 1985
   February 7, 1988
   May 23, 1989
   October 16, 1989
   April 27, 1990
   May 24, 1990
   June 22, 1990
   July 8, 1994

A brief biography of Andrew Jackson 1767-1845, at
http://odur.let.rug.nl~usa/P/aj7/about/bio/jack08.htm

The American Presidency, Andrew Jackson, at
http://gi.grolier.com/presidents/ea/bios/o7pjack.html

Florida Governors' Portraits, Andrew Jackson 1767-1845, at the internet site
of The Division of Historical Resources, Florida Department of State,
See: http://dhr.dos.state.fl.us/governors/jackson.html

Andrew Jackson and Florida, at
http://www.gms.ocps.k12.fl.us/florida/bios/jackson.html

In addition to published sources, the author is deeply indebted to the
following who helped me gather insights into the Barkleys and their
world, and who provided motivation to move this work from family
history and isolated stories into a single cohesive publication.

The late Adelaide Rutherford Willis
The late Rosalie Willis Tate
Rev. B. Madison Currin, ThD.
Clara Garnier Minnich
The late John Daniels
Sandra Johnson
Nancy Fetterman
Dr. John Cavanaugh
Richard Brosnaham
Archivists for the City of Pensacola
Archivists for Escambia County, Florida
Archivists for the Pensacola Historical Society
Dr. Judith A. Bense
Dr. Margo Stringfield
Ted Nickinson
Dr. Jack Fleming